A HAND -BOOK TO COFFEE PLANTING

IN SOUTHERN INDIA

A HAND -BOOK TO COFFEE PLANTING

IN SOUTHERN INDIA

JOHN SHORTT

GYAN

Published by

Gyan Publishing House
5, Ansari Road
Daryaganj, New Delhi-110002
Phone: 011-47034999, 9811692060
E-mail: books@gyanbooks.com

Distribution Network
gyanbooks.com
India, USA, Canada, UK, Australia

ISBN: 978-93-6780-297-7 (HB)

First Published, 1864

2nd Impression 2024

Printed at: Gyan Press, Delhi.

A Hand -Book to Coffee planting in Southern India
Author: JOHN SHORTT

A HAND-BOOK TO COFFEE PLANTING

IN SOUTHERN INDIA,

BY

JOHN SHORTT, M. D., M. R. C. P. F. L. S.

MEMBER, LICENTIATE OF MIDWIFERY AND DENTAL SURGERY OF THE ROYAL COLLEGE OF SURGEONS, ENGLAND, FELLOW OF THE OBSTETRICAL, ETHNOLOGICAL, ZOOLOGICAL, AND ANTHROPOLOGICAL SOCIETIES OF LONDON, AND LOCAL SECRETARY TO THE ANTHROPOLOGICAL SOCIETY FOR SOUTHERN INDIA, &c., &c.

AUTHOR OF THE PRIZE ESSAYS

ON

INDIGO AND COTTON, &c., &c.

H. M. MADRAS MEDICAL SERVICE.

ZILLAH SURGEON, CHINGLEPUT.

MADRAS:

PRINTED BY PHAROAH AND CO.

ATHENÆUM PRESS.—MOUNT ROAD.

1864.

TO

HIS EXCELLENCY SIR WILLIAM DENISON, K. C. B.,

COLONEL ROYAL ENGINEERS,

GOVERNOR OF MADRAS,

THIS SMALL VOLUME

OR HAND-BOOK OF COFFEE PLANTING,

IN SOUTHERN INDIA,

IS BY PERMISSION

RESPECTFULLY DEDICATED,

BY THE AUTHOR.

PREFACE.

In launching this work on Coffee cultivation before the Public, it will be necessary to explain what claims I have to consideration on this subject, and from what sources I have obtained my information, since planters will no doubt be disposed to enquire what experience I can have had in coffee planting. As I am merely an amateur planter, *my experiments* extend over a few plants only which I have for some years carefully cultivated, and watched their habits and constitution, but my observation extends over some millions of plants, not only in the so-called planting localities, some of which I have visited, but in various parts of India I have observed the habits of the coffee plant, in amateur experiments similar to my own.

Horticulture or Agriculture is a practical and not a theoretical science, and theory although very well in its place is worthless in itself, when not borne out by practice and experience. Practice without theory is but hap-hazard work, but when theory is tested by practical experience and based on science, we cannot go wrong, for we know and understand the subject in all its bearings, and can practically carry out the teaching of theory and the facts of science, in our Horticultural and Agricultural operations.

The cultivation of coffee in this country is now attracting much attention, and being carried out on an extended scale, to meet the demand which is constantly increasing. We hope that in the absence of a better, this book will be a guide to those entering into coffee speculations, and may prevent the loss and misdirection of labour consequent on capital imprudently laid out. There are numerous localities, soils, hill sides and plateau, still lying waste or overgrown with jungle, which are admirably suited for coffee, and which with a moderate capital judiciously laid out, might be converted in to smiling plantations giving handsome returns. The chapter on the "Physiological consideration of the coffee plant," might be made applicable to almost any plant. The object of considering the subject here and confining the observations entirely to coffee, was with a view of impressing the subject on the mind of the planter, and to give him an interest in the study of the plant itself. Having always been fond of Horticulture and Agriculture, for the last 6 years I have made it a special study, during my leisure moments, and the knowledge thus acquired I have fully applied to the subject under review, and have not only given the results of my own observations and experiments, but have taken advantage of every work I could procure, so as to bring together as far as possible, all that has been written on the subject.

Whilst in the midst of my M.S., I was by the kindness of the Honorable J. B. Norton favored with the perusal of Laborie's and another pamphlet, a reprint from the "*Ceylon Observer*," containing "Letters on Pruning" by W. and the manuring of coffee estates by C. Wall, Esq., and as I have not acknowledged these in the body of the work, I have much pleasure in alluding to them here.*

I am in an especial manner indebted for much valuable information to my friend H. G. Morison, Esq., who has been familiar with coffee planting from his boyhood; for from the time he landed in this country after completing his education, he has been more or less engaged as a planter and merchant.

Mr. Morison is not only a planter, but a successful one. and from his familiarity with most of the planting localities

* These pamphlets have since been reprinted by Mr. Higginbotham. Bookseller and Stationer, Madras.

in Southern India, he was in a position to afford me valuable assistance, and readily placed the information he possessed at my disposal.

My obligations are also due to B. A. Daly, Esq., who has been a coffee planter on the Shervaroy Hills for the last 22 years, for much information. I am greatly indebted to W. H. Staines, Esq., of Coonoor, for specimens of Insects, and for having placed at my disposal some valuable "memoranda" bearing on the subject of coffee.

I have also to thank Messrs. Fischer and Co., of Salem, and General Ottley, for various hints on the subject of coffee cultivation, &c.

To my friend Mr. G. Norton, the Chemist and Druggist, I am greatly indebted for having so kindly and readily undertaken at my request to analyse not only the ash of the plant, but the soil also.

I am aware that this work falls short of what it might be, but as my sole object has been to assist those engaged in a subject which seems to have become a mania of late, I ask the indulgence of the reader for any shortcomings that may be found in the body of the work.

JOHN SHORTT.

CONTENTS.

CHAPTER I.

CHAPTER II.

CHAPTER III.

CHAPTER IV.

CHAPTER V.

CHAPTER I.

Coffee.—The Coffea Arabica belongs to the natural order Rubiaceæ, or Cinchonaceæ, the Pentandria Monogynia of Linnæus ; which contains many species of "berry bearing tropical shrubs."

* "The natural order Cinchonaceæ consists of trees, shrubs, or herbs with simple opposite leaves ; interpetiolar, glandular stipules ; cymose inflorescence. Calyx adherent, entire or toothed ; Corolla regular, stamens attached to the Corolla. Ovary 2 celled, style 1. Fruit inferior separating into cocci, or indehiscent and dry or succulent, seeds definite and erect, or ascending, or indefinite and attached to a central placenta embryo small in horny albumen."

"The Coffea Arabica, from its being the principal producer of coffee, is the chief and most useful, but besides this, other species are cultivated in other parts of the world,on account of their commercial value ; all of which although now regarded as separate species, owe their origin to the Coffea Arabica, which was first introduced into Arabia about the commencement of the 15th century, from Enárea, and Cáffa, in Southern Abyssinia, to which countries it is indegenous."†

The coffee bush is a pretty, evergreen shrub, varying from 15 to 20 feet in height. The flowers are white, with a slight rosy tint; and emit a strong jasmine odour. The fruit is a succulent berry, about the size of a cherry, and

---

* Balfour's Botany, page 829.

† Beverages we Infuse.—Blackwood's Magazine, No. 459.

contains two seeds which are hard and horny, and are now universally known as coffee beans. We have so little acquaintance with the fruit of the coffee previous to its preparation for the market, that comparatively little is known of it beyond the appearance it then presents, and the delicious beverage it yields, which is too well known to require detailed notice here; although little more than two centuries have elapsed since its first introduction as an article of commerce, and the hospitable cup of the Arab first spread its charms into English homes. It is said that a Molah named Chadely was the first Arab who used coffee, which he drank during his nightly devotions to keep him awake. His disciples followed his example; its stimulating properties soon became known among pilgrims, who in their peregrinations introduced it into Medina, Mecca, and finally throughout Mahomedan countries.

According to all authentic accounts, coffee was first introduced into Europe at Venice in 1615, reached Marseilles in 1654, and was taken direct to Paris from the East by Solyman Aga in 1667. The first Café was opened in Paris in 1669, by an Armenian named Paskal, who not succeeding there removed to London, where he opened a coffee-house in George Yard, Lombard-street, which was such a success, that in a twelve month there were as many coffee-houses in London as in Cairo.

Another version is, that in 1652 the first coffee-house was opened in London by a Greek named Pasqua.*

European nations have adopted the use of this mild stimulant to such an extent, that its consumption far exceeds that of tea, and in proportion as the demand has increased so efforts have been made to extend its cultivation to different places in the torrid zone, with what success we shall

* Blackwood's Magazine, No. 459

presently see. Arabia long preserved a monopoly in coffee, and but for the exertions of the Dutch and British, we should have been forced to rest content with the scanty supplies afforded by the little hills of Mocha. It is related that in the midde of the 15th century, the Kadi of Aden, Abd el Kadir, Mahomed el Aza ri'el Jeziri el Hanbali, having occasion to visit Abyssinia, found coffee in general use there, and on his return introduced the plant into Aden, from whence it is supposed to have extended into Mecca, Egypt, and eventually into Europe. An Arab named Sheikh Ali Shaduli Ibn Omar introduced it into Mecca.* It was introduced into Ceylon by the Arabs, prior to the invasion of that island by the Portuguese. The Dutch introduced the coffee plant into Batavia in 1690, and at the same time commenced its cultivation in Ceylon. On the cession of this territory by the Dutch, its culture was continued by the Cinghalese, and during the British occupation of Ceylon, the Mahomedan inhabitants bartered its produce at Galle and Colombo. The introduction of the coffee plant in the West Indies, is traceable to a single tree sent as a present to Louis 14th of France, by the Magistrate of Amsterdam. Cuttings from this tree were sent to Martinique, where it soon became established, and was the means of extending coffee cultivation all over the West Indian islands.

The introduction of coffee into the East and West Indies, Java, and Ceylon, has proved of great benefit to the public.

The credit of having established the first upland plantation in Ceylon in 1825, is due to Sir Edward Barnes,† who thus gave that impetus to coffee cultivation which has caused it to be produced in such large quantities, that the stock on the 30th June 1862 in the United Kingdom, and

---

* Balfour's Cyclopædia of India, 2nd Supplement, page 147.

† Balfour's Cyclopædia do. do. do. page 147.

principal Continental ports, may be estimated at nearly 60,000 tons.

United Kingdom	9,550
Holland	27,750
Antwerp	3,400
Hamburg	9,500
Havre	5,900
Trieste	3,470

I shall now endeavour to describe the modes of cultivation of the plant, confining my remarks more especially to cultivation of coffee in India. To consider the subject fully and in all its bearings, it is necessary to divide it into the following parts.

1. History, climate, soil, coolies, felling, roads, nurseries, seeds, marking off plantation, pitting or holing, transplanting, weeding, vacancies, trenching, terracing, catch drains, &c.

2. Pruning, based on the Physiology of the plant.

3. Physiological considerations of the plant.

4. Chemical analysis of the ash of the plant and soil, &c., &c.

5. Manure based on the constitution of the plant.

6. Cost of planting, with particulars of the chief localities given.

7. Diseases, insects, and animals destructive to the plant described.

8. The Medicinal, Chemical, and Physiological properties of coffee considered.

9. The collection of the produce and preparation of it for the market.

10. Various resources of a plantation. Coffee leaf tea, its preparation, Chemical Nutritive and Physiological properties. Manufacture of spirits from the pulp. Infusion of the pulp, husk, &c., &c.

11. Aroma of the coffee bean.
12. Statistics of coffee.
13. Stock yard.
14. Hints to Planters on the preservation of their health, and that of their Establishment.

Before discussing these subjects, it will be as well to review the cultivation of coffee in its native clime, and in its natural state. Now we know as a fact, that the Arab does not generally sow his seed in order, or establish nurseries, or otherwise attend to the welfare of the plant, until it attains maturity. The seed is simply scattered, and the plant germinates fostered only by the hand of nature and watered by the dews of heaven, yet it grows luxuriantly, frequently attaining from 15 to 20 feet in height, and producing largely. When the fruit is ripe for gathering, camel hair mats are spread beneath the trees and the ripe berries shaken off. The fruit is collected and dried in the sun in the berry, and when perfectly dry, the husk or dried skin, and membrane are separated from the fruit,by pounding in wooden or stone mortars. In this manner is prepared the Mocha long berry, and the deformed and rounded bean known as the "pea berry," which command the market, and place it out of the power of the most cultivated and carefully prepared coffee to vie with them.

"In the interior of Arabia there are hill villages maintained solely by the produce of their coffee, which is grown on Terraces, and planted so densely that the rays of the sun can hardly penetrate the groves. Although for the most part coffee in Arabia is not irrigated, but made dependant on the rains, in these parts some of the plantations are systematically watered by means of large reservoirs formed on the heights, in which spring as well as rain water is collected, and distributed over the terraces ; and the coffee thus watered produces a second crop in the year, but the fruit only ripens well during the first crop, whilst that of the second is cast away in an immature state, and is consequently always inferior to the first."*

"Coffæa," Niebuhr says, "was brought from Abyssinia to Yemen by the Arabs, from a country similar to their own plains and mountains. By that people it has for ages been cultivated in the hilly range of Jalab, watered by frequent rains and abounding in wells and tanks. Here the plants are grown in grounds that are continually irrigated, in soil from 1 to 1½ feet deep. The climate is rainy from June to September. Fruit begins to ripen in February (terraced and irrigated.) Little more is known, unless we add temperature.

March—7 A. M. . 69° to 76° Fahr.
1 P. M. . 85° to 95°
10 P. M. . 73° to 81°

Richness of soil in the West Indies is said by some to cause inferiority of quality, and to the supposed dryness of Yemen has been ascribed the excellence of Mocha coffee, but it has been shown that the Arabs abundantly irrigate. The point to be attended to is, to select a climate where the heat of tropical plains is counteracted by elevation, where during the dry season water can be commanded, and especially where the air is clear and cloudless and Irrigation abundant."†

"Coffee in Arabia is irrigated with care, the water, being turned off as the fruit ripens; lest it be rendered too succulent."‡

The European planter, on the other hand, selects a forest situated at a medium altitude of about 3 or 4000 feet above the level of the sea, and having cleared his land and pitted the ground generally transplants seedlings, which have been

* "Travels of Roland," translated from the French by Cecil Hartley, A. M., 1853.

† Penny Cyclopædia, Vol. vii. page 321.

‡ Bingley's Useful Knowledge, Vol. 2, Page 21.

nursed with care for a season or two, and placing them from five to six, and sometimes seven feet apart, awaits with anxiety the appearance of the first blossoms

Little further is done on the plantation at this early stage, beyond keeping it free from weeds, and this even is not done by all. During the second year trenching is practised, and if circumstances prove favorable, the plants grow healthy, and sufficient care be given them, a fair crop is generally produced in the third year, which with ordinary care ought to yield from 4 to 5 cwt. per acre.

The cares and anxieties of the planter now commence; he watches with anxious solicitude the timely rain for the forming of blossoms, by which his prospects for the ensuing season are determined. Light showers in May generally help to push forward the blossoms, and should these not be succeeded by a drought but by other timely showers, the plants are invigorated and the fear of failure removed. About the time that the blossoms are forming on the coffee bushes, the S. W. monsoon generally sets in, followed by heavy showers of rain, which continue more or less up to the end of October, and in some distrcts this is followed by the N. E. monsoon, which frequently continues up to January.

About the end of November, the planter makes preparations for trimming up the plantation. Extra labourers are now employed, and weeding is carried on. In a well organised and regular plantation, this is a trifling operation, but where the place has been neglected and allowed to run wild, it becomes formidable.

The Pulping house and drying grounds are now looked after, and set in order for the forthcoming harvest.

December brings with it the ripe coffee berries, sometimes a little earlier or later. Labourers are daily sent out to gather the ripe fruits, which are kept overnight, and pulped the next morning. The pulper is a simple roller covered with copper or zinc sheeting. A piece of wood is screwed on parallel to the cylinder, with just sufficient space left between the two to admit of the coffee bean deprived of its pulpy covering, passing through without being crushed. The berries are placed in troughs over the cylinder, which is made to revolve, and as the fruit passes through, the pulp is freed and thrown on one side, whilst the coffee bean falls on the other, and is frequently conducted on to a cistern filled with clean water, and freely agitated to deprive the seeds of their mucous covering, in which they remain some 12 or 18 hours, each planter being guided by his own views on the subject. When the seeds are taken out of the cisterns, they are placed either on paved drying grounds, or on platforms covered with bamboo matting, where they are allowed to dry, for three or four days, and are then called parchment coffee.

The next process consists of freeing the seeds of their parchment or membranous covering, which is rudely accomplished by pounding the seeds in a mortar, or on the ground. To the latter method many object, as it discolours and imparts an earthy flavour to the coffee.

A more simple and widely adopted plan for freeing the seeds of their parchment, is by means of what is known as the "*trough*;" it consists of a circular groove lined with wood or stone, into which a large wooden or stone wheel is fitted, and worked by human or animal power, the wheel moving round and round in the groove, after the fashion of a mill. The groove is filled with the parchment coffee, which is freed of its covering by the pressure and rotatory motion of the wheel.

When the bean is taken out it is winnowed, by throwing up the seeds against the wind, and the coffee is finally picked clean of foreign bodies, and stored. Another more complete machine is used on a few estates for pulping coffee, and is known by the name of "Meacock's Patent." This machine consists of two heavy pieces of wood or metal, placed together like grinding stones, their faces spiked closely with iron wire. To this mill a rapid rotatory motion is given, by a wheel moved by cattle in a circle. Whilst the parchment coffee is placed in a feeding trough, and enters the mill in the required quantity, the cleansed bean falls through the apparatus into a receiving box, where fans are placed which effectually winnow the berries, which then pass through a wire sieve placed on an inclined plane. The object of the sieve is to separate the beans of unequal size from the large ones, as it has been found that in roasting coffee the smaller beans are burned or charred, ere the larger ones are half roasted.

I have here briefly reviewed the system of cultivation and preparation of coffee, as practised in Arabia and East India. I believe the same system is carried out in all parts of the world, perhaps in some instances a little modified, to suit peculiarities of climate, soil, or other local circumstances.

The Arabian coffee still maintains its superiority, depending no doubt on some peculiarity of soil, and the climate being congenial to the growth of the plant, whereas in other climates the cultivation is in a measure artificial, and the climate and soil tend much to modify the peculiar aroma of the berries. The qualities and aroma are not only dependant on the ripeness of the berries, but the particular mode of curing the bean, and the effects of climate and soil affect its commercial value.

The following is a list of valuation for coffee in the London market, on the 1st September 1862.

1 Mocha..................	100 to 112s. per cwt.
2 Jamaica	87 to 112s. per cwt.
3 Cuba	81 to 92s.
4 Costa Rica.............	80 to 90
5 Ceylon..................	70 to 100

6 Mungerabad	92/6	to	99
7 Wynad	85	to	92
8 Lackady.			
9 Bahia	52	to	65
10 Native Ceylon	70/6	to	71
11 Rio	77—bought in.		
12 Shervaroy	80	to	90
13 Malabar and Mysore	70	to	100
14 Batavia	67	to	87
15 Brazil	60	to	85
16 Singapore and Sumatra	56	to	72s. per cwt.

From the foregoing it appears, that the wide differences we perceive in coffee produced in various parts of the world, are not to be ascribed to any one reason in particular, but that, climate, soil, elevation, culture, &c., all combine in determining its commercial value.

It may be useful therefore to examine each subject separately, commencing with the climate and soil, and taking up in order the different agricultural operations necessary to the successful cultivation of the plant, and the collection and preparation of the produce.

Climate and Soil.—The coffee plant requires a damp or moist climate. It luxuriates in places where torrents of rain descend, such as the slopes of hills and vallies ; nothing is so fatal to this plant as a drought. Both experience and science teach us that with the necessary amount of moisture, all vegetation requires a sufficient quantity of heat, to maintain it in health and to favour the ripening of the fruit, and it has been repeatedly ascertained by experiment, that the coffee plant does not thrive in cold climates ; it has even failed on the coldest part of the Neilgherry range of hills, near Mungerabad, where although it grows luxuriantly, the fruit is cast away in an immature state, and never arrives at maturity, from the want of sufficient warmth.

Places subject to dense fogs continually covering the hills, are equally objectionable, although a moderate quantity is desirable, as mists and heavy dews supply moisture, and tend to refresh and invigorate the plants during the hot weather. In the selection of a locality, therefore, too much attention cannot be paid to each of these points; for we frequently see instances in which planters take up land and prepare it, without previous examination of its position and suitability, and discover when too late, that some great defect exists in the climate, that completely unsuits it for the cultivation of coffee.

The next requisite for the successful growth of coffee, is the soil. This should be rich, abounding with moisture, and containing much humus or vegetable mould, consequently we find the plant thrives best on either red or black clay, containing combinations or preparations of iron, and covered over with humus formed by the decay of vegetable matter produced by dense forests. When these points are overlooked, the results are soon seen in the rising plantation.

The planter, perhaps, instead of choosing forest land, has taken up a poor, grassy, or stony situation, and however much water he may have access to, his plants are stunted and soon become yellow, unless he resorts to heavy manuring at a very early stage, which materially increases the expense of the concern.

In hard or rocky soils, the pits require to be deeply excavated, to permit of the tap roots of the plant striking perpendicularly down, and even when every precaution is taken, it will be found that estates opened out on poor soils will always prove more expensive than those on forest land, and are not so lasting.

The berry produced on rich ferruginous clay, is found to contain more aroma and the bean is heavier, when compared with those of other localities. This fact is so well known to coffee brokers generally in London, that a new importation is frequently weighed after being roasted.

If we take a view of the W. Ghauts on which are embraced some of the finest coffee growing districts, we find the Neilgherries, Wynad, Mysore, Coorg, Mungerabad, and the Shervaroys, all contain in a greater or lesser degree, the requisite properties, and when these are wanting to any extent, high and expensive cultivation is necessary to remedy such defects.

The productions of the two largest coffee districts of Java and Ceylon, which regulate the market, are grown, we find, on cleared forest land, and the soil approaches in elevation to that of India.

This is a consideration that should on no account be overlooked. The pine of the Himalayas will not thrive in lower latitudes, nor does the Teak of the Forest succeed on snow clad hills, and in like manner coffee requires for its proper growth, and maturation, an elevated soil, and when we depart from its natural range, the plant degenerates.

From 3 to 5,000 feet above the level of the sea, and at a proportionate distance from the influence of sea breeze, seems to be the situation in which coffee thrives best.

Above or below this height, the tree may thrive, but it produces fruit scantily, and is subject to injury from extremes of heat or cold.

In the low countries there is not sufficient moisture in the soil, and when shaded and irrigated, it produces a coarse and uneven bean, devoid of the peculiar aroma essential to good coffee.

The improvement that has of late years taken place in every branch of agriculture and horticulture, and the advantages derived from it, are so well known, that we can in no way be surprised at its application to coffee growing.

A coffee plantation should be attended to as an horticultural undertaking, for each individual plant requires looking after, and careful nursing; and I feel assured that if capitalists who enter on this speculation would only study the subject scientifically, and practice the rules of horticulture in the undertaking, the results of their operations would prove much more successful than they do at present.

The planter must not only be possessed of capital, but requires nice judgement and practical skill, combined with a little common sense, to carry out the work before him, but these are not all. He must be in the enjoyment of robust health, to be able to withstand the deadly effects of a damp atmosphere, for in all probability he will have to spend his time surrounded by the direst malaria, out in the open air from morning till night, supervising the work in course of operation on the estate; for where this is not done, it is sure to be inefficiently carried out.

Coolies.—In the employment of coolies, powerful and healthy men, if possible from among the hill tribes, should be selected, if any be procurable in the vicinity, as they are the most expert in the use of the axe, &c., particularly; but they require close and careful supervision. There should be a maistry to every gang of 20 coolies; the maistries being held responsible to the superintendant for the work done by the gangs under their charge. On all estates task work should be introduced, in preference to any other system, so that each individual executes a fair proportion.

Where coolies have to be procured from a distance, too much care cannot be bestowed on their selection, subsequent housing, tendency to fever, &c. This disease should thus be checked at the outset, in doing which the planter will not only be serving his own interests, but those of humanity also.

Coolies in strange places are erratic and unsettled in

their habits, and consequently cannot be depended on for continuous labour; but will in such cases require kind treatment and persuasion, to keep them at work. Experienced labourers will perform twice the work of inexperienced ones, and stand the climate better; they only require careful management.

In establishing a coffee plantation, the first thing to be considered is the selection of the locality, bearing in mind the necessary conditions of the soil and the requisites of *Climate;* that is, the various conditions of temperature, atmospheric pressure, humdity, rain fall, &c. These points having been considered, the planter sets to work by felling or clearing the forest; which should be commenced early in the year, as it is the most expensive part of the undertaking.

Felling.—Good virgin forests should be selected, although it has been proved within the last few years, that thick Bamboo jungle yields splendid crops of coffee. This or other land having been selected, the planter commences clearing the land by felling trees, &c.; beginning in time to finish the process of felling by the end of the year,—always employing experienced coolies. There are two modes of operating: 1st by completely felling the trees, and subsequently destroying them by fire or otherwise removing them from the land.

The second by partly destroying the trees, and then setting fire to them; each of these two methods we shall now consider.

In following the first plan, all the undergrowth in the shape of weeds, long grass, shrubs, &c. should be first cleared, and if on a hill tract, it should be commenced on the lowest part; this effected, trees should be half cut, beginning on the same spot, and cutting as close to the ground as the play of the axe will permit; a large tree should then be selected in a commanding situation, and at a certain height, so that in its fall it will bring down all in its vicinity; on a hill side where the forest is dense, if a good leader in the way of a giant tree be chosen, and all below it cut partly, the entire slope can be felled with facility, each tree throwing down the others before it.

The hill tribes in the jungles of Orissa are very expert in this work. A gang of coolies should follow the fellers to lop off the branches, and clear the trunks of the fallen trees to facilitate subsequent burning.

The other mode consists of cutting a groove the depth of two inches round every large trunk, so as to separate the alburnum and sap wood; in a little time the trees wither, and the bark above the groove becomes detached—the trees are then set fire to, the bark, boughs, twigs and leaves are burnt away, leaving the trunks alone standing. These in course of time are either felled for timber or subsequently fired at the roots, thrown aside, and allowed to decay. The standing of the naked trunks in no way impedes the work of pitting, &c. for planting. According to the former plan, the fallen timber is burnt off the soil when dry, which usually takes place in the course of 3 or 4 months; but this plan is open to objection, as burning the prostrate timber cakes and hardens the soil, and at the same time destroys a large amount of organic matter, whereas in the 2nd plan the heat is thrown off the ground into the atmosphere, and the subsequent slow destruction of the wood by decay is far more beneficial to the soil, than the small quantity of minerals left by thorough incineration, as is more generally practised.

It would be more desirable to let the timber rot slowly on the soil; it will thus form a more valuable manure than any got by burning. To adopt which, all the branches, &c. should be arranged in parallel rows between that of the plants, and the shelter from this source alone will suffice to protect the young plant from the heat of the sun. Although burning the land is beneficial on certain soils, it is not so on coffee land, for vegetable mould, the very material required in abundance, is liable to destruction by such a process.

Roads.—As soon as the land has been cleared, roads should be laid out. Their number and width should be determined by the size of the plantation. Besides one or two main roads, there ought to exist a number of feeders, and should the plantation be on a hill side, the gradient should be made as easy as circumstances and local facilities will admit; a good bandy road is a great desideratum, besides which, the plantation should be traversed by bridle tracks on all sides, converging towards the centre, and communicating with each other. The Estate having been pretty well cleared, its particular form marked out, and roads laid out, nurseries should be established.

Nurseries.—This being the first step to be taken, it should engage the planter's attention early. In some districts, facilities for purchasing seedlings may exist, but in all cases these should not be depended on.

Frequently much time is lost in getting up nurseries, and as a season is an object to the new planter, he often buys plants for the first year until his own are ready, and in this case the most healthy looking plants should be chosen.

In establishing nurseries, care should be taken to choose a well drained spot, not dry, stiff, and clayey, but one with a light, free and rather moist soil. The ground thus selected should be within the limits of the plantation, or as near to it as possible.

Should the choice fall on a Hill slope, the higher it is situated the better. Under these circumstances, level ground with facilities for irrigation, in the shape of streams or other reservoirs, should be selected. The land should be thoroughly ploughed up or trenched with the mamooty, to the depth of 18 or 24 inches, and all the weeds exterminated thoroughly, when it should be freely manured at the rate of from 3 to 5 tons per acre, levelled, and squared into beds, after which it is ready for the reception of the seeds.

Seeds.—Much care is necessary in the selection of seeds, which should be taken from vigorous, healthy plants. The berries intended to supply the seeds should be well formed, and the produce of trees averaging from 7 to 10 years of age. They should be fully ripe when plucked off the branches, and be sown when fresh, at a depth of one inch, and dibbled in the soil in drills 10 or 12 inches apart from each other, so as to give the plantings plenty of room to grow, and subsequently enable the planter to remove them with facility from the nursery to the plantation; or the seeds may be sown in drills, and as the seedlings begin to grow, the drills should be thinned out to the same distance. The seeds may even be scattered broad cast in the beds, and as they sprout should be thinned out to the regulated distance; care should be taken to let the plantlings grow free of each other, which will make them vigorous.

It is not necessary in all instances to put down seeds fresh, as, if well dried and preserved in closed vessels, they will keep fresh from 3 to 6 months. As soon as the seeds are sown, they should be watered sparingly, and the beds lightly covered with straw, rubbish, &c.*

Coffee seeds at best are slow in germinating;† I find that they very seldom come up under three weeks or a month.

---

* The fruits should be broken up and the seeds in their parchment sown singly, as each fruit contains two seeds generally, and if the cherry be placed in the soil entire both will grow together like twin plants and may cause difficulty in transplanting subsequently.

† NOTE.—In Carraccas, seeds are germinated between plantain leaves, and are supposed therefore to stand the sun better—crop of 3rd year is from 1 to 1¼ lb. per tree.—HUMBOLDT.

The plumule or young stem shoots out of the soil, the seed lobes unexpanded, from an inch and a half to 2 inches, and it takes from a week to 12 or 15 days before the first pair of seed leaves are unfolded, and, nearly a month after before a second pair of leaves expand. The seedlings should be irrigated from time to time as may be required. This should be done generally in the evening, and the seed beds should be artificially shaded from the midday sun for 4 or 6 hours during the hottest part of the day : if not protected, their tender leaves are liable to get scorched by the direct effects of the sun, and they should be free from overhanging trees, to avoid their drippings in case of rain. But this shading should not be carried on to too great an extent, as in that case the seedlings will grow lanky and delicate, unable subsequently to withstand the heat of the sun. The planter's best attention should be given to the nursery, for on the health and vigour of the seedlings will in a great measure depend the success of the future plantation. Each individual plant will require frequent examination and every encouragement given, by frequently loosening the soil lightly around the roots, to promote vigorous growth. The seed beds ought to be frequently weeded, and the first weeding should take place as soon as the young plants begin to appear.

When the nursery has supplied the plantation, the remaining seedlings should continue unmolested in the nursery beds, for they can be used to fill up vacancies, and by such a course, the age and size of the plants on the plantation will be in keeping. The stems of the seedling plants are cut down, when they are termed in planter's parlance "*stumps*" or *stools*." In transplanting these, greater care is necessary, in consequence of the greater size of the ball of earth that will have to be taken up to prevent injury to the roots. It does not seem generally known that the coffee plant can be as readily propagated as the Cinchona, which under the able superintendence of Mr. McIvor has been wonderfully multiplied. Coffee belongs to the same family as the Cinchona. My experiments prove its success, but I claim no originality in the matter for it has been long known, and was the only way in which the coffee plant was introduced into Martinique by the French, but as the seeds are abundant, planters may not care about extending coffee plantations by cuttings and buddings, yet the fact should be more generally known.

Propagation by cuttings should thus be carried out ; nursery beds similar to those described for the reception of seed having been prepared. The cuttings which should have a diameter of ⅓ or ½* inch, and be from 5 to 8 inches in length, should be planted out in the beds. In placing the cuttings in the soil, they should be placed somewhat obliquely, so as to favour the ready ascent and descent of the sap, and in from 1 to 3 months roots will have formed. They will require the same care as that given to the young seedlings, till they have been fully established in the soil ; or the planter may with perhaps less trouble resort to what gardeners term layering. Should it be decided that layering should be practised, the planter or superintendent goes round and selects two or more layers from the most healthy and vigorous plants ; he here bends over and buries into the soil some 4 or 5 inches of the branch, to facilitate the descent of the roots as well as to arrest and concentrate the sap. At the part placed in the soil, the lower part of the bark should be slightly roughened or scraped, or a slight cut in the wood, so as to divide one-third of the circumference of the stem,

---

* NOTE.—Since the above was written I find the following in Paxton's Botanical Dictionary for 1849—Article Coffea. "The coffee tree is a very ornamental plant succeeding well in peat and loom, and if kept clean and free from insects it will flower and fruit abundantly ; to grow well, it must have a *good supply of water* and plenty of pot room ; *cuttings of the ripened wood root readily in sand*, under glass in a moist heat." The italics are mine.

should be practised. By adopting this system, in from one to three months the layers will be found to have rooted and established themselves in the soil—when the connection between the parent tree and the layer should be divided, and in about a month or 3 weeks from the division the layers will be ready for transplantation. The advantage of layers consists in being able to select our layers not only from the most healthy and vigorous plants, but also the most prolific can be selected, for it will be found that some trees produce much more largely than others, not only in the quantity, but also the aroma and form of the bean can be better propagated in this manner—at any time of the year.

In the formation of some estates, where the land is very rich and moist, instead of forming nurseries, the seeds are planted out on the estate itself. When this is done, pits about 2 feet in diameter and from 18 to 24 inches deep are excavated, and filled up again with soft vegetable mould, and in each of these pits from 2 to 3 seeds are dibbled in to about an inch of the soil, and the distance of an inch apart, and as they sprout up, the healthiest are left and the others pulled out, or transplanted to spots where the seeds may have failed to germinate, or have been destroyed by accidents. This is not a bad plan to be adopted on good rich soils, for the plants grow up healthy and vigorous, and the growth is not arrested as is the case, for a short time at least, when transplanted. Nevertheless, transplantation is preferable, for the change of place decidedly benefits the plant when once it establishes itself in its new locality, and pushes out with great vigour should attendant circumstances prove favourable.

Marking off the Plantation.—Every thing on a plantation should be carried out scientifically, order and regularity being studied in all cases, no matter how trifling they may appear. The beauty of the plantation should be looked to, as well as its productiveness.—The first thing to be done with a view of excavating pits for the plants, is to mark off the spots, at the regulated distances, in straight lines. For this purpose cords, pegs, and wands are necessary. A good number of pegs, or stakes from 4 to 5 feet in heighth, are requisite, besides several pieces of cord, each 100 or 200 feet long, numerous wands, each 6 or 7 feet long, a mallet or two, the necessary instruments for excavating, and the required number of coolies.

A piece of cord is stretched out in a straight line, with a cooly holding either end, which they tie or fasten to a peg driven for the purpose; a wand is laid at either end, and a second cord stretched out as before, at the regulated distance. Guided by the wand, when this is done, they may go on laying down as many lines as they have cord sufficient for, and then return to measure off the distances by the wands of 6 feet each, where either a peg is driven, or a piece of scarlet cloth tied, marking out the spot for excavation.

The distance at which the pits should be dug, must in a great measure be decided by the nature of the soil; if this is dry, 6 or 7 feet apart, but if moist, 9 or 10 feet will not be too much. The plants should be quite free of each other when full grown, but in a dry soil they should just meet.

To save time the cords may be previously marked off, by tying pieces of rag or coloured cloth at the determined distances, and on the cords being stretched, the cooly passes on with stakes and mallet, driving a stake on the inner side of the rope at every piece of cloth he comes to.

To render the plantation more regular, lines might be stretched across the previous ones, should there be much cord at command. By the aid of the wands, lines are laid down either way; the squares thus formed by the cord receive a stake at each angle. Difficulties may exist in consequence of irregularities of surface, steepness of hills, &c. in laying out the lines, but these can be at once remedied or avoided by an intelligent superintendent. If a sufficent number of wands of the proper length be given to the markers, the lines will be perfectly straight and the distances regulated.

Pitting or Holing.—As soon as the ground has been correctly marked off, holes must be excavated at each of the spots where the stakes were driven ; in doing which care should be taken not to displace the stake, as it will form the centre in which the plant should be placed. If the stakes be drivin 3 feet in the soil, they will remain undisturbed by the excavation. Each pit should be three feet in diameter and 36 inches in depth, and should the soil not be rocky, a single cooly will in a day of 10 hours excavate from 30 to 40 of these, 35 being the average. Coolies should be provided with sticks of the determined length and breadth of the hole, to guide them in their work, and at the close of each day, or before the work is resumed the next morning, the pits should be carefully examined by the superintendent, to see that they are of the proper breadth and depth.

In making holes, cubes of 3 feet deep are the best, for we should remember that in most places the surface soil is seldom deeper than 18 inches or 2 feet, when we may come on hard gravelly or stony soil, which may tend to arrest the growth of the plant. The deeper the pits, so much more vigorous will the plants grow. The holes should now be filled up with vegetable mould, decayed leaves, and soft earth, with a superficial dressing of manure, and they will then be ready for the reception of the plant.

Transplantation.—In consequence of the slowness of growth of the seedlings, it will take from 8 to 16 months before they are sufficiently advanced for transplantation. Under no circumstances should plants be taken up ere they are at least 8 or 12 inches in height.

The best time for planting out is after the first burst of the monsoon, or else the soil becomes so saturated with water, that it rots the new roots the plants attempt to throw out in their new situation, and this will soon prove the death of the seedlings. Care should be taken that no water stands around the plantings for the first month at least, unless the season is dry.

By the retention of the stakes in the holes, there will be no difficulty in maintaining straight lines in setting the plants in the pits.

Advantage having been taken of the most favorable time for removing the plants from the nursery for planting out, the most healthy plants should be taken up with a ball of earth to each, and should the soil not be sufficiently adhesive, it should be tied around with straw, grass, weeds, &c. and be carefully laid in a basket, which is carried as it is filled to the planting ground by a cooly who deposits a plant to each hole, whilst another places them carefully in the holes, which are previously filled with surface soil. In doing this the plant should be held perpendicularly in the left hand, the surface soil carefully placed round it, and the whole be gently pressed down with the feet, care being taken to give the seedling its proper direction in keeping with the line.

In placing the plants in the holes, their roots should in no way double, but should just rest in the surface soil thrown into the bottom ; and every care should be taken not to break or otherwise injure the roots, but should such an accident unfortunately occur, they should be cut off clean at the injured part. Should the sun be powerful, the plants will require protection for a few days, which might be done by planting a good branch above each, and should the rains fail immediately after, it will be prudent to water the plants occasionally.

Weeding.—This is the next operation that will have to be attended to after transplantation, and perhaps no operation is so much neglected.

Most of the plantations I have seen in this country, are covered with weeds and coarse grass, in the greatest profusion, and if the plantation happens to be young, from this cause alone many young plants are choked up and killed; in addition to this they breed vermin, and insects which soon attack the coffee plants and destroy them, and from their giving cover to reptiles of various kinds, are likely to endanger the lives of coolies, and other servants belonging to the estate.

It should be remembered that all vegetable substances derive their nourishment from the soil, and by the overgrowth of foul weeds a large proportion of the nutritive elements of the soil are wasted, to the injury of the coffee. It stands to reason that two plants growing in a given locality will take up more nourishment than one, and the plant which grows up the sooner will exhaust the greater part of the nourishment, so the slow growing plant will be deprived of its nutriment by the fast growing weeds.

The presence of weeds on a soil not only destroys the moisture of the soil, but deprives it of certain elementary matters that accompany it. For instance, if two plots of ground be selected and weeds allowed to grow on the one, and the other be kept clear of weeds, it will be found that all the moisture from dew, &c. is dissipated from the blade, in the spot grown with weeds, and the nourishment lessened by them; whereas in the plot free from weeds, the earth will have absorbed all the dew, &c. that falls, and the soil will be materially enriched by it. The truth of this can readily be ascertained by a rude chemical experiment. On some plantations grass is allowed to grow, and cattle to run loose; the grass is grown to furnish fodder for cattle; now this system is decidedly objectionable, for in the first place the soil is not only impoverished by the growth of grass, but the plantation suffers from cattle being allowed to run loose. It is true that cattle do not eat the coffee plants, but by brushing past the trees, and on any alarm by rushing wildly and trampling them, they injure the plants, and when in blossom they throw down many of the flowers and of the young fruits. Buffaloes in particular are fond of rubbing themselves against the stems of plants, by which they not only break branches and twigs, but frequently denude the stems of their bark, to the great injury of the plants : this subject will be again taken up elsewhere. Should the ground at the onset be thoroughly and completely freed from weeds (although it may be a considerable expense it will be found in the end a saving), there will be no difficulty in maintaining the plantation free from weeds, for one coolie will be able to keep clean and manage from 3 to 5 acres ; after this, no weeds should ever be allowed to seed on a plantation ; before they blossom, if not earlier, they should be uprooted ; if this system be strictly carried out in the course of 2 or 3 years the plantation can without difficulty be kept in an exceedingly clean state, to the great advantage of the planter.

The secret consists in not merely cutting away the heads of the weeds, as is practised on most plantations, for this only adds to the vigour of the "*shoots*" that are left, and causes them to spring up with greater luxuriance, but the roots must be grubbed out.

All uprooted weeds should be at once transferred either to the trenches or to the main dung pit, to form manure : allowing them to lie about the plantation exposed to the sun, some of their volatile constituents are likely to be dissipated by the sun's rays. They may also be allowed to dry on the soil, previous to being burnt, when their ashes form good manure. Some planters are in the habit of burying the weeds, either at the root of the coffee plants or in their vicinity, which is decidedly objectionable, as it breeds insects and is likely to destroy the plantation ; besides which, by the large amount of carbonic acid some weeds exhale, the coffee plant may be poisoned, and the great heat caused by the decomposition of the vegetable matter is likely to kill it. Weeds then are found to render a plantation sickly, to stunt the growth of the plants, and to make the leaves grow yellow by depriving them of their requisite nourishment and moisture. When plantations have become overrun with weeds, their clearance will entail much trouble and expense, more particularly when they are of some extent. In these cases I find it much better to thoroughly cleanse a small portion at first, and if necessary a second and third time.

If this plan is not followed, before a few acres are got over the weeds will spring up so rapidly, in the portions first operated on, that it will be as bad as ever by the time you finish. When thoroughly cleansed this will not happen, at least so rapidly.

In weeding, attention must be paid to the situation of the plantation ; if in a flat valley, it will be the better for free delving, but if on a hill slope, delving would help to wash away a large part of the soil, consequently here simply scraping away the weeds and grass should be practised, and only those weeds which have taken on woody stems will have to be dug out, after which the soil should be beaten down. Loosening the soil is of great advantage to the plant itself, enabling the rootlets to strike out, and the stem to expand, thus giving health and vigour to the plant, therefore the soil should be kept as loose as circumstances will admit. It should be the planter's constant care to keep the plantation thoroughly clean. Six or Twelve thorough weedings annually will be sufficient. Weeding should be commenced at one end, and carried on through the plantation from end to end.

Vacancies.—Now is the time to fill up vacancies that may have been caused either by failure of the plantlings originally placed out, or by accidents, &c. &c. All sickly plants should be removed, and their places filled up by fresh healthy plants from the nursery. It should be borne in mind that the younger the plant is, the greater is the facility for transplanting. Most planters are fond of removing large or full grown plants, but they require great care in their removal, and from the depth to which the roots will have entered the soil, they will be more liable to injury in removal. On a well managed plantation, vacancies will seldom occur.

Trenching.—The system of trenching has of late years been recommended by a Mr. Wall of Ceylon, and when the trenches are properly excavated it is no doubt an advantage, in some instances being as useful as terraces, in preventing the soil being washed away during the rains; and at other times the trenches will answer the purpose of refuse pits, into which all refuse matter, whether animal or vegetable, and the weeds from the vicinity, may be thrown. No matter for what purpose intended, accumulations of these should be removed to the dung pit before the setting in of the rains. The advantage of this is, that all the water from the surrounding surface will be drained into these trenches, and thus a large portion of the soil otherwise likely to be washed away, will be deposited in the form of fine silt, which might be subsequently taken up in deepening the trenches when choked up. It will then prove a valuable manure for the coffee plants, as it contains rich fertilizing matter.

The usual trenches are from 5 to 6 feet long, about 2 feet wide and of a proportionate depth, but they might be cut of length and depth according to the planter's fancy, and the labour he can command for the work. The water, as it falls into these trenches, allows of sufficient time for the deposit of all its mineral or earthly constituents, ere it again flows off from the surface of the pits; in fact they act the part of strainers in only allowing the fluid to run off, and retaining all the solid matter it contains. This practice is so well understood by natives in general, that in filling their stone-built tanks, or water reservoirs, the streams are not allowed to enter the tanks direct, but are guided to a cistern first, where, as the water settles, it flows on to the reservoirs, freed in a great measure from its impurities: were it not for this; the tank would soon become choked up with silt, whereas by having a cistern, this is deposited in it, and it is annually cleared out at less expense than it would have cost to clear the tank, had water been conducted directly into it.

Terracing.—Where plantations are situated on the steeps of hill sides, terracing has been practised with the same object as trenching; viz., to prevent the soil being washed away, but trenching where practicable should always be preferred, as its advantages are greater, for not only is the soil prevented from being washed away, but it is collected in the trenches in the form of compost, and forms valuable manure, besides which, the expense and labour are not so great as in terracing.

Unless the terraces are well and carefully built, they are likely to be washed away or otherwise destroyed,* but in certain localities this system possesses advantages; the planter can only decide whether trenching or terracing will be most suitable, after examination of each individual locality.

As to those who doubt the injury done to plantations by the washing away of the soil, I have only to ask them to examine the subject practically, ere they give an opinion.

By examining the different streams at Chingleput and the Shervaroy Hills, I found that every gallon of water after a heavy shower of rain carried away from ½ to 1 ounce of soil, independent of such ingredients as were dissolved by the water. These proportions vary in different localities.

It should also be stated that the soil contains several saline materials essential to the growth of the plant. These are readily taken up by water, some in large, others in small quantities; thus many of the elements necessary to be retained in the soil are carried away. This, by careful trenching or terracing, can to a great extent be prevented.

These saline materials are noticed in connection with manure. To prove this point, let a determined quantity of water be evaporated in an evaporating dish, and the saline materials can be discovered by the microscope from the crystallization, and from the particular form of crystals, the various salts may be made out. My experiments on a rude scale at the opening of the monsoon, gave 5 gr. to every 40 oz. of water on the Shervaroy Hills, but this quantity became much less eventually.

Catch Drains.—These should be opened out in all directions, and conducted in the first instance to the different trenches, from whence they should be guided to the rivulets or streams on the hill sides. They should not be of any depth in the first instance, but merely to guide the surface water into the trenches, to prevent the soil being washed away, as this is of the utmost importance. The number of drains will depend on that of the trenches, and should the soil not be hard, it will eventually prove to the benefit of the planter to take advantage of the services of the coolies occasionally, to have these paved with stones.

The best way of doing this is to tell each gang of coolies off for so many drains, on which they are to work in their leisure hours, and a small present should be promised for each one completed. These drains should be from 1 to 2 feet in width and depth, and the gradient should be guided in a great measure by local circumstances. Surface soil washed away from any part of the plantation, should be carefully collected from the different streams after the cessation of the rains, and either alone or mixed with manure used to cover the roots of the plants.

Forking.—On some Estates, what is termed "forking" is practised, which is certainly much called for when we remember how the plantation is trampled upon by pickers, pruners, and weeders, so that it is a wonder how the trees exist, for the soil around them is rendered stony and hard with all this trampling. "Forking" consists in simply turning the soil with steel forks to the depth of 8 or 12 inches, where the soil will admit of it. In some parts of Wynaad, pickaxes are used for the same purpose, either because they have no steel forks, or because the ground is too stony. At Coonoor, Mr. Staines is able to fork an acre at from 5 to 7 rupees; a most useful operation, when we consider the vigour it gives to the plant by loosening the soil around it. These forks are known as 'Parke's 4 pronged forks."

CHAPTER II.

Pruning.—Pruning consists of various operations connected with either arresting the height of the plants, to cause them to spread out laterally, or to remove the additional growth of wood, and thus encourage the plants to push out new fruit bearing shoots. These various operations come under the different heads of topping, pruning, and handling, each of which we shall now consider successively.

Stopping or topping, is an operation practised to arrest the growth of a plant, so as to dwarf its height and enable it to spread out laterally; the object gained is two-fold,—by dwarfing the plant we establish it securely in the soil and prevent it being injured by storms or strong blasts of wind, and at the same time we facilitate the operation of picking the crops, as the pickers will have the berries within reach.

There is a difference of opinion among planters on this subject; some being for, and others against it, but it is undoubtedly called for on all plantations that lie exposed and are likely to suffer from gales, &c., but in sheltered localities it does not matter so much, though it will save a good deal of trouble, for ladders will be required to pick the fruits off untopped trees. The topping and untopping of trees should be considered with reference to the situation of a plantation, the distance of the plants from each other, &c., but topping undoubtedly increases the vigour and out spread of a plant, and at the same time it throws out so large a number of shoots as to choke the crown and thus deprives the plant of the free circulation of light and air, and frequently causes it to run into luxuriance of wood and foliage, unless the plants are carefully attended to.

Should it be decided that the plants are to be topped, and the height at which it is to be effected having been considered, wands of the intended height, 5 feet in length, should be prepared and distributed among the operators to commence operations, as far as my own experience goes, when the wood is under a year's growth. I find it best to use a sharp knife, and to nick the stem at the regulated height on 4 sides, when the stem being bent on the knife comes clear off, and will leave a tolerably clean surface which should be covered with a mixture of cowdung and clay to prevent the evaporation of the sap. The cutting should invariably be performed at 2 inches above the joint. A hand saw should be used when the wood is above a year old, and care be taken not to shake the tree so as to disturb the roots in the soil. If a chopper be used, the wood is frequently split up along the stem and injures the plant very materially—but under a cautious and careful superintendent almost any instrument may be used—but on large estates where it is almost impossible to give the plants that close attention, the work must in a great measure be left to coolies, who by their careless manner of working may injure plants.

It is always better to stop trees when they attain the requisite height, than to allow of their shooting up much beyond it, for then the tops are so tender and brittle that they can be pinched off with the fingers while the wood is green, and even if a knife be used no concussion ensues and the plant is scarcely disturbed. After the top has been taken off, the crown should be squared at the top by pinching away the tops of all branches ; those near the stem shorter than those at a distance ; and every branch or shoot from and around the main stem should be removed, to the extent of 6 or 8 inches, and the root stem be kept free to the extent of one foot above the soil.. Immediately after the fruiting season is the best time for topping plants, as nothing need be done until the first crop has been gathered. Many planters sacrifice the first and sometimes the second crop either wholly or entirely, but this is a point on which no general rules can be laid down ; the locality, soil, and climate must be considered, but if these crops appear to be unusually large, the trees are likely to be weakened and their boughs may also give way from over weight : in such cases it will be advisable to sacrifice the partial or entire crop.

There are then two principal objects to be borne in mind with reference to topping, viz., to give security to the plant in the soil against wind and storm, and secondly to give facility to the collection of the crop. Of the two, the latter is the more important, for it applies without reference to locality, whereas in the former locality is the chief point on which the question turns.—Admitting that weapprove of and actually practise stopping, we should next turn our attention to pruning.

Pruning as the word is properly used may be practised by any one ; but to do it scientifically is another question, for the tree should not be mutilated, while at the same time all superfluous as well as unproductive wood should be removed, and fresh fruit bearing branches encouraged to take the places of the unproductive ones.

We should now call to mind the conformation of the plant, to which we shall allude when discussing the "Physiological consideration of the coffee plant."—Coffee plants throw out branches or shoots invariably in pairs, and these pairs are at right angles to each other—this is a provision of nature peculiar to the plant, and when we find it otherwise, it is owing either to accident or to destruction caused by birds or animals. If we closely examine a coffee bush, one of the two shoots or branches starting from either side will be frequently stouter and stronger than the other, and from the nourishment being directed more largely to it will be found to produce a greater quantity of fruit. On the other hand the opposite branch will be found weak, and the wood itself will not equal that of its fellow either in girth, strength or productiveness. We should take advantage of this fact, by cutting off the latter branch at from 2 to 4 inches from the laterals or primaries, thus every other branch should be cut away on opposite sides. This will to some extent check the vigor of the plant and establish it the more firmly in the soil, and the further advantage gained would be to cause the stump to throw out fresh shoots ; one or more of the vigorous, if allowed to remain, will push forth its twigs and concentrate its sap so as to bear fruit the following year ; this is what is termed in planter's language "pushing new wood." These branches are termed "secondaries," and the shoots that spring from them are termed "tertiaries." A further advantage gained by topping off every alternate branch, without reference to its strength or weakness, from each joint, is to lighten the plant and allow of the free circulation of air and penetration of light between the branches of the plant, and thus to render it much more healthy and vigorous. This alone will suffice for a second or third year's plant, but older trees will require the same operation more or less modified according to the wants of each plant. This operation will strengthen the branches as the previous operation does those of the stem.

It must be remembered that the very fact of topping plants will make them throw out an infinite number of shoots, so as to crowd and prevent the tree from having access to air and light which are so necessary to its health and vigour, and it will also exhaust the vitality of the plant in sappy wood and luxuriant foliage, at the expense of fruit, unless freely handled.

When plants are topped lower than 5 feet, there is no room for the play of the new shoots that push out, and the consequence is, as may be seen on plantations, the crown is matted with wood—on the contrary by stopping a plant at 5 feet, and keeping the root stem one foot above ground free of shoots, there will be a surface of 4 feet on the main stem, to allow space for the play of the shoots and the crown will in no way get matted. Therefore pruning is actually called for, and I cannot do better than give a few succinct rules for the performance of this operation.

Vide Illustration.

5 feet.

2½ feet

2½ feet

a. Stem or main trunk.
b. Lateral primary, or first branch.
c. Secondary or branch of first branch.
d. Tertiary or branch of second branch.
e. Cut secondary.

2. By stopping your plants at 5 feet, they will become vigorous, by foreshortening the laterals at 2½ feet, over much drooping is prevented.

3. Never cut a lateral, but keep them clear near the stems, to admit light and to allow of the free circulation of air, otherwise they grow lean and often wither away.

4. Soon after a secondary has borne crop, cut it at about 2 nodes or joints from the point of the primary, but leaving the opposite secondary for the next year for pruning. When the secondary is cut away, the stump shoots out afresh, and in the following year a crop will be the result.

5. Remove all tertiaries, as being useless to the plant, and only tending to impoverish it by the quantity of wood they push out. The simplest way is to either pull away gently the tertiaries at the different nodes, or cut them off carefully without injuring the secondaries.

6. By cutting the secondaries every other year alternately, you will not sustain loss of crop.

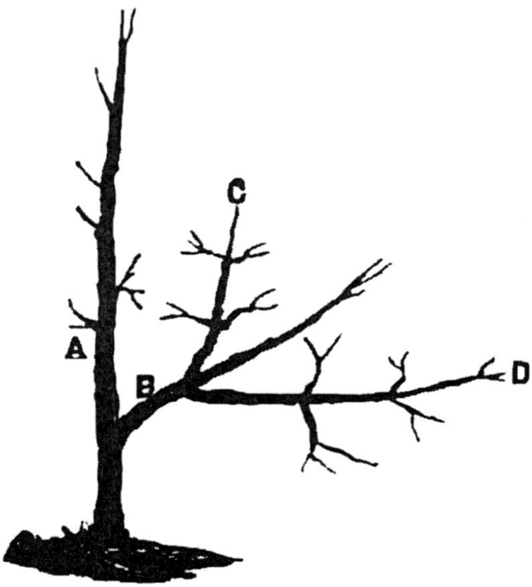

a. Stem. *b.* Lateral.

Thus, cut this year at *c*, and next year at *d*—and so on.

7. Remove all branches with the knife, that grow into the crown, or are irregularly thrown out and cross each other much.

8. Keep your plants short by topping them at about 5 feet, and they will become vigorous and healthy.

9. All broken or otherwise injured branches, should be carefully cut away from the coffee bush. If these rules are carefully adhered to, we shall seldom go wrong on the subject of pruning.

Handling.—We now come to the last operation, namely, that of "*handling*." Handling means the examination of the plants by the hand, and the removal of all superfluous shoots, which can be better done by removing and plucking them away with the hand from the base. No "*stump*" or "*stool*" is left for the reappearance of fresh shoots, the wound readily heals, and all is over. The stopping the growth of a plant, induces it to burst forth in all directions with young shoots and suckers, that will so crowd and choke the crown of the plant, as completely to exclude light and air, consequently handling will be called for to remove these, more especially to keep the centre of the trees carefully clear of young wood.

Another advantage gained by handling when properly performed, consists in passing the hand lightly along the stem of the plant, not only to remove suckers, but to clear it of moss and other parasites and at the same time free the stem of any loose bark; for this only gives cover to insects in most instances destructive to the plant itself. But this operation should be effected very gently. It is however all very well to sit down and write rules: the difficulty arises in these cases from the want of command of intelligent labour, for no rule however explicit will be found to answer so well as a practical knowledge, and everything which we do on a plantation, should be done with some definite object based on scientific principles. For not only should the desired object be gained by topping, pruning, and handling, but the eye should be pleased with the regularity and order in which these various operations have been carried out. In this will be seen the results of scientific planting as opposed to other systems—as is seen in the work of a mechanic, in which it is the finish of the work that shews the hand of the master mechanic. The same rule may be applied to the planter, for each individual plant will require a different system from the main in topping, pruning and handling, in which it will be necessary for the Planter and his Superintendent to use their judgment, according to the wants of each plant.

The proper season for pruning, is as soon as the crops have been taken off the plants. The crops will ripen from September to January, but from the want of labour it may be prolonged to March, and sometimes even to the middle of April, when before the coolies disperse, pruning should be carried out, not nominally but scientifically, so as to remove every useless branch or twig, and give vigour to the plant and enable it to push out fresh fruit bearing shoots ; and even the handling should not merely be confined to the suckers, but the entire plant should be examined, and every sucker or other unprofitable wood removed. Whilst the pruning is being carried out, a cooly should follow the footsteps of the pruner with a composition made of equal parts of clay and recent cow's dung, a little of which should be spread over every wound made by pruning or handling. This will prevent the evaporation of the sap, or in other words will prevent the plant from bleeding which would weaken it, and will sometimes proceed to such an extent, as to sicken the plant and cause it to die eventually.

CHAPTER III.

Physiological Consideration of the Coffee Plant. —The planter will find it of great advantage to be acquainted with the functions, on which the life and duration of plants depend.

The great mistake made by planters in general is, in considering their operations *Agriculturally*, instead of making them a strictly *Horticultural process*, for not only does the plantation as a whole require attention; but the most assiduous care must be paid to each individual plant.

" That *Horticulture* should be successful, it must be a close and intelligent imitation of nature; though within certain limits, some variations, in keeping with the character and habits of the plant, may be introduced."

" The *secret* of successful *Horticulture* is an acquaintance with the *laws* of vegetable growth, obtained through the aid of science; thus *Botany* has contributed in elucidating the theories and facts of vegetable Physiology. *Chemistry* has given valuable assistance by the analysis of various soils manures, &c., and *Meteorology* comes to the aid of the planter, with apparatus of a varied nature, for the purpose of taking down observations, and thus all combine to enable him to carry out his operations on a scientific basis, and a correct estimation of these facts will ensure success, and every process conducted on this basis will in all probability secure a higher development of the plant."*

Plants, although incapable of motion, are endowed with

* Illustrated London News.

life, and posses the various functions of growth, formation of secretions, reproduction, and decay, which are analogous to those of animals ; but they differ from the latter in not being gifted with perception and voluntary motion.

The *Reproductive Process* in the lower order of plants, is carried on by means of the same kind of cells which answer to all their other functions.

But in the higher order of plants, we have this process maintained by a compound and more highly organized medium—the seed—which contains within it the vitality and germ necessary for continuing and propagating the particular species to which it belongs. Such then is the coffee seed, which, will if we examine carefully, be found to contain, within it the germ, so small as to be scarcely perceptible to the naked eye, surrounded by a kind of horny albumen, which forms the essential part of the seed we term "*Coffee.*"

The seed contains not only the germ, but a sufficient store of nourishment for the support of the young plant, until such time as the seedling is able to imbibe nourishment from the soil, and carry on an independent existence.

The only requisites for germination are, that the seed must be placed in a favourable locality, surrounded by a certain amount of heat and moisture, and be accessible to air.

The horny substance of the coffee seed for the most part is made up of fine cellular tissue, or a massy network of cells, the sides of which readily admit moisture by a process termed endosmosis—or suction—into their interior, with the assistance of heat, the water at once dissolves the contents of these minute cells and causes a new and peculiar process to take place by which oxygen is absorbed and carbonic acid exhaled ; the starch which the cell contains is dissolved and converted into a liquid composed of gum and saccharine matter, to supply material for the future sap of the plant. This transformation could not take place unless the starch had parted with a portion of its carbon ; but now a process whereby carbon is fixed and oxygen is set free is also necessary to the welfare of the plant, and for this purpose darkness is requisite, as it has a tendency to fix carbon.

Nature abounds with the elements necessary for the maintenance of vegetable life, and the plant has only to extract from the soil such of these elements as are necessary for its own peculiar form of growth ; but as different parts of the soil do not contain the elements necessary to every form of vegetable life, and as climatic and atmospheric peculiarities differ also, so, certain kinds of plants only, will thrive in particular localities.

When plants are grown in soil which does not contain the elements necessary, or if the supply of them is exhausted or is scanty, they soon either perish or become sickly and stunted in growth, or otherwise diseased.

Under these considerations we find, therefore, that coffee will only thrive in certain climates, and in a certain latitude, and here only put forth its whole strength in attaining perfection. Notwithstanding this, its physical or vegetative, stamina is so great that it may be grown anywhere—but to make it "pay", the necessary pabulum for the plant should exist in the soil, the temperature be mild, and the atmosphere loaded with moisture : without these favourable conditions, the planter may in vain explore new localities or expend capital and skill.

Coffee requires an altitude of from 1,000 to 5,000 feet above the sea level. Anything above or below this range will not suit its growth, in one case from excess of moisture and excessive coldness of the atmosphere being present, and in the other from want of moisture and the great aridity of the temperature ;—both extremes therefore are preventives to its success.

Should attendant circumstances prove favorable to its growth, the coffee seed, when sown, should sprout out in, from 3 to 6 weeks, sometimes earlier, but seldom later.

When the seed begins to germinate, it first absorbs moisture from the soil, swells, bursts its seed coat, and is seen to rise out of the earth enclosed in its parchment, whilst the radicle enters the soil: it is as yet dependent on the horny albumen of the seed for its nourishment; but in a week the seed lobe enclosed in the parchment will have exhausted its store of nourishment of gum and sugar formed from the starch, and the radicle will have thrown out fibrous threads, and the root as a whole now assumes its function of extracting its own support from the soil. By degrees, the seed lobes by exposure to light and air become vascular, expand, throw off their membranous covering, assume a green color and become what are termed seed leaves, and imperfectly perform their function of supplying the plant with nourishment—till succeeded by others.

The seed leaves are more or less oval and gradually become dark green by the fixation of carbon, the upper surface of the leaf which is exposed to the sun is membranous, the epidermis or outer covering is dense and transparent.

On the under surface the cuticle is thin and transparent, and is full of openings, by which moisture and the principles of the atmosphere so necessary to vegetation are absorbed. This pair of leaves is now in a condition to elaborate the nourishment which the young roots are able to draw from the soil, and add to the strength and vigour of the plant, which they do through the medium of a particular apparatus attached to their extremities, called spongioles.

The seed leaves are opposite and form the first joint, from between them the plumule is continued in the form of a sharp point, which gradually opens out into a pair of lance shaped leaves: these are the first pair that take on the true form of the leaves.

At a distance varying from one to two inches, the different joints are successively formed, as the plant increases in age and size, and continues to extend, throwing out pairs of leaves at each joint and from these joints, branches also start, arising from between the leaves in pairs, one on either side of the stem, from the axillæ of the leaves, thus forming crosses at right angles to each other.

Or, in Botanical language, the leaves and boughs are said to be opposite and alternate, or both leaves and boughs form a spire around the stem. Nodes or joints are the points to which the leaves are attached by their petioles or leaf stalks. These knotty points are well seen in the coffee plant, and the spaces between them are termed internodes. In the nodes, the bundles of wood are compressed and turned aside from the axis, so as to enter not only the leaves but to form a point for the starting of branches, in the formation of leaf buds ; whilst in the internodes, the woody fibres rise perpendicularly, lying parallel to each other.

The essential part of a node is the new disposition given to the woody and other tissues to meet not only the wants of the leaves, but those also of the future branches, by the termination of the growing process, and is directed towards the formation of a leaf bud at the base of each leaf. This process, in planter's language, is called the "pushing of new wood," and will be alluded to again when on the subject of pruning.

The stem of the coffee plant consists of *three parts* ; namely, the outer covering termed *bark* or *skin*, the internal mass of *cellular* tissue termed *pith*, and between these the woody fibre called *wood*. On examining a transverse section of the stem, we see in the centre the remains of the pith, next to it the layer of woody fibres, and enveloping the whole, the bark.

The woody fibre will be found arranged in concentric

layers, marked by a series of lines or rays which pass from the centre to the circumference, or as it is more scientifically expressed, there is to be seen the pith, wood, medullary rays, and bark.

The pith forms the centre of the stem, and consists of loose cellular tissue, from which run outward in all directions lines called medullary rays. It becomes gradually absorbed as the plant grows, so that after a certain time, no vestige of it remains in the lower part of the stem, but at the upper part it may be recognized by the central spot which the wood surrounds in circles, and it may be seen in young shoots, showing as it did at the first formation of the plant, but it is not to be found in the roots.

It is continuous with every other part, branch, leaf bud, and flower, and forms the chief organ of nourishment and depository of all the secretions. It also maintains a direct connection with the bark through the medium of the medullary rays, forming the centre of the horizontal system for the formation of the sap, and performing those important functions on which the life of the plant especially depends.

The wood is hard and knotty, and is the part that gives stability to the plant. It forms the substance of the trunk, and is generally laid out in a very regular manner, the woody fibre forming distinct zones, each being the produce of a year, having a dark tint near the centre and becoming lighter towards the bark. The outermost zone is that of last year's growth, and the inner ones of the preceding years, and these are seen very distinctly in the coffee plant; they are formed by the leaves during the growth of the plant, and descend to the root between the bark and the wood which has been previously formed, by which we learn that the stem has increased in size by additions on the outside, owing to which the name of *Exogen* or outside growth is given to plants which increase in this manner.

The quantity of woody fibre that forms annually, will depend chiefly upon the number of leaves, and these will be in proportion to the size and luxuriance of the plant—an increase of growth takes place annually most probably, until the plant attains its maximum growth, depending more or less on the varieties of the soil, peculiarity of climate, seasons and winds.

The bark is the outer covering of the plant, and is of a grey color, and is compact in structure, being more or less rough, and divisible into several layers. First we have the cuticle or most external layer, which is continuous with that of the epidermis of the leaves—secondly we have what is called the corky layer of the bark, this generally continues firm around the stem, but occasionally it cracks and even peels off at intervals, owing probably to the increase in size of the stem during the warmer seasons—Thirdly we have the most internal layer, the "Liber," which is found placed in small bundles; it is the vascular layer, and is very strong;—externally it is in contact with the corky layer already alluded to, and by its internal surface it rests on the smooth wood.

The bark is useful in giving protection to the wood, and in further elaborating the "Cambium" or formative fluid from which all the tissues of the plant are developed. This fluid is found most abundant in plants during the season of spring. Thus the bark is found necessary to the life of the tree, from its connection with the cellular system.

By the number of air and other vessels which it contains, it not only conveys the refuse matter from the leaves to the soil, but is also a depository for the secretions of the plant.

Roots.—We now come to the roots; that part of the plant which enters and fixes itself in the soil. That of the coffee is what is called a "Branched tap root," which terminating in branches and rootlets, penetrates the soil to the depth of from three to five feet, according to the particular nature of the soil on which it is grown—and which is in keeping with the stem and its branches, for as the one developes and spreads upwards, so the other becomes developed to the same size in the soil.

The roots will frequently be seen to deviate from the perpendicular, should they meet with stones or other obstructions in their descent into the soil, or when in search of better soil.

The "Collum" or neck, is the name given to that part immediately above the soil—and from which the stem starts upwards and the roots downwards. The roots form a kind of wedge, from the nature of the surface they have to penetrate.

Their extremities are not only minute, but are constructed of a most delicate structure, the spongiole, which was spoken of in a previous part, and which by an inherent vitality is enabled to insinuate itself between any resisting substances, as stones, &c. and is the principal part by which all fluids which enter the plant are admitted, consequently it is of the utmost importance in transplanting young plants, to avoid injuring too many of these delicate organs.

Organs of Fructification.—These consist of the *flower* and the *fruit*; the flowers are small and white, forming clusters around the branches of each joint; the flower stalks, or peduncles are short, and support the calyx or outer floral covering; the corolla or flower leaves, form stamens and a pistil. The two last constitute the sexual organs, those parts intended for the purposes of reproduction. The stamens are the male parts of the flower and the pistil the female part.

The seed is the essential part of the plant, and is formed last; it is of the highest importance, and in this particular plant, from its commercial value, it should be the produce of vigorous and healthy plants.

Nature with her many resources preserves the seeds of plants with the tenderest care, so we find that the coffee fruit, from being what is termed a berry, is carefully protected by a soft pulpy substance, and surrounded by a corcaceous membrane. The young fruit is first seen in the shape of a knot, (at which time the corolla which is deciduous falls away, whilst the whole of the pistil is persistent and falls when the fruit ripens)—and gradually increasing in size, changes its color from green to yellow as it approaches maturity, when it becomes matted with reddish spots and streaks, and eventually takes on a deep purple hue, falling to the ground when perfectly ripe.

The mature fruit is first covered with a thick tough skin ; it has next a dense coating of a sweetish mucilaginous substance, and next to that a tough membrane termed the parchment. This parchment is so tough and firm, that it protects the coffee from destruction and preserves its vitality, for when the fruit is eaten by animals or birds, it passes through without its vitality being in the least impaired. In each seed, the seed lobes or organs of nutrition are found.

If man's first study was directed to such substances as served him for food and clothing, his attention was doubtless subsequently drawn to the cultivation of articles conducive to his comfort and luxury, and as his social position improved, he naturally surrounded himself with such comforts and luxuries as were attainable by him. Coffee may be considered as an important item in the many productions of the vegetable kingdom which in one form or another contribute to his gratification and enjoyment and add to the increase of commerce.— *Ward.*

Coffee has risen so high in the estimation of all nations,

and during the last few years its cultivation has been extending so very widely in all parts of the world favorable to its growth, that there is little chance of its losing its popularity through any change of either fancy or taste.

CHAPTER IV.

Chemical Analysis of the Coffee Plant.—It is now generally understood that plants withdraw certain constituents from the soil; these are both inorganic and organic, and give to each particular kind of plant the constitution necessary to enable it to sustain vegetable life.

The produce of any piece of ground, depends in a great measure on the materials required for the particular kind of produce. Although for instance rice, or other grain or vegetables, exhaust a field, the cultivator does not suffer from it, because he gains a large return by the produce, and is thus enabled to restore to the soil in the shape of manure, the materials exhausted by the crop.

This he can do more effectually and economically, when he has ascertained by chemical analysis the food required for the particular crop he chooses to cultivate, even when it is not grown as food but as a luxury of civilization. Thus when Indigo or cotton forms the subject of cultivation, the object kept in view is in the one case to increase the development of the coloring matter, and in the other to improve the staple and quality; to do either of which, particular elements are required, and when these have been withdrawn and the soil impoverished, they must be resupplied in the shape of manure. The planter must follow in the footsteps of the agriculturist, and supply to the soil the elements of the produce which he obtains in the shape of coffee.

It has now been clearly established, not only by chemists but by the investigations of other scientific savans, that certain vegetable subtances are not the result of formations abstracted from the soil, but are that of the vital action of the plant upon the constituents of the atmosphere, which we know consists of oxygen, hydrogen, nitrogen and carbonic acid.

These elements, as they constantly exist in the atmosphere, form the constituents of gum, sugar, &c., whilst the oxygen evolved by the vital action of plants, by the fixation of carbonic acid, purifies the very air we breathe. We have in those elements the materials for sugar, &c., formed independently of the soil, it is still requisite that, to maintain a plant in health and vigour, it should draw nourishment from the soil, which it will thus exhaust.

In coffee the valuable part is the bean or seed, and the richer this bean is in aroma and flavour, the more valuable it becomes.

The chemical analysis has never been satisfactorily conducted in this country, and the one or two English formulas are I believe obsolete. Being anxious to determine this question, and not having myself the requisite facilities for conducting an examination of the kind, I engaged the services of my friend Mr. Norton, late Assistant to the Professor of Chemistry, who kindly undertook the work, and the materials for the analysis were supplied by me, every precaution being taken in preparing the ash of the plant. A full grown coffee plant, supposed to be 10 years old, loaded with flower and fruit was uprooted. The plant had grown under the shade of a mangoe tree, and was consequently somewhat lanky; it stood 15 feet in height from the soil, on the 8th November 1862. The stem was double, and simply adherent; when taken up it separated into two parts, indicating a twin origin; at the surface of the soil, the right division of the stem measured in circumference 8¼ inches : and the left 6¼ inches : the entire plant weighed 17¾ lbs. avoirdupois, viz.,

	lbs.
Weight of root stem with roots, &c......	7¾
Central stem........................	7¾
Leaves, twigs, fruits, &c................	2¼
Total lbs....	17¾

The plant was cut up, the wood tied into a bundle, the leaves, twigs, fruits, &c., were secured in a calico bag and daily put in the sun to dry ; on the 19th January 1863, when reweighed, the result was found as follows :—

Root and stems........................	9¼ lbs.
Leaves, twigs, and fruits................	1 „
Total....	10¼ lbs.

The dried wood, roots, leaves, twigs, fruits, &c., were now placed in a clean, new earthen chatty, and thoroughly incinerated ; on the same day, the ash that was left weighed 6 oz. 5½ drams.

Per centage of composition of plant.

	lbs.	oz.	drs.
Water lost by drying...........	7	8	0
Organic matter..............	9	13	10½
Ash......................	0	6	5½
Total..	17	12	0

The ash was now secured in proper stopper bottles and submitted to Mr. G. Norton for analysis.

The several processes adopted by Mr. Norton in the analysis were in accordance with those laid down by Frezenius, in his 2nd edition on quantitative analysis, section 212. Mr. Norton states,— "I scrupulously adhered to the instructions therein detailed." The results are satisfactory.

Composition of the coffee plant ash, in 100 parts.

Potassa	15·	76
Soda	18·	98
Lime	26·	07
Magnesia	4·	26
Sesqui oxide of iron	9·	22
Phosphoric acid	13·	28
Sulphuric acid	2·	79
Chloride of Sodium	8·	35
Silica	1·	29
	100·	0·0

We are quite ignorant as to how the mineral constituents essential to the vitality of plants, exist in their organisms; that they are not combined in the form obtained from their ash is generally admitted. Our ignorance in this respect, however, in no way affects what the progress of science has shown to be the most eligible form for adding them, when required, to the soil; the soluble condition is that which is aimed at, or one nearly approaching it. Although the benefits obtained from the chemical analysis of plants are by many misunderstood, and therefore occasionally considered not essential for success this is only thecase to a certain extent because we practically carry out manuring and are often put to considerable expense from not knowing the required wants or elements of the particular plant, whereas by analysis we at once ascertain the nature of these with certainty; for as different species of animals require different sorts of food, the same is the case with plants. It is frequently difficult by analysis alone to calculate its money value, or to seek a remedy to correct the known defects of the soil, nevertheless even in this instance there are so many practical facts drawn out by analysis, as to tend to correct practical appliances.

"About 1849 Mr. Herepath gave the following analysis of 150 grains of fine, West India coffee berries, for the purpose of determining the best manure for the West India coffee estates. Deducting the carbonic acid, 100 grains of ash gave

Phosphate of lime	45·	551
Phosphoric acid	12·	801
Potash	16·	512
Soda	6·	787
Magnesia	5·	942
Lime	2·	329
Sulphate of Lime	1·	751

"It would appear from the *Bombay Standard* (1859) that in a subsequent communication from Mr. Herepath, dated 13th June 1858, addressed to Mr. Walters, a chemical analysis of Ceylon coffee he reports that 1,000 pounds of raw coffee berries of Ceylon plantation's growth contained the following mineral ingredients—

	lbs.
Potash	37
Lime	$2\frac{3}{4}$
Magnesia	$5\frac{3}{4}$
Per oxide of iron	$0\frac{1}{4}$
Sulphuric acid	$2\frac{1}{2}$
Chlorine	$0\frac{3}{4}$
Carbonic acid	$11\frac{3}{4}$
Phosphoric acid	7

and he mentions phosphoric acid, sulphate of lime, and carbonate of magnesia, as the principal ingredients required for manure.—About 100 lbs. of Peruvian guano, with 7 or 8 lbs. of ground gypsum, 10 lbs. of magnesian limestone mixed with Ceylon vegetable mould, or the ashes of the wood clearances and some pounded granite or quartz, would make good manure for 1,000 lbs. of raw berries."* It is generally believed that coffee is not an exhausting crop, but there can be no doubt that it does exhaust the soil, when we glance over its constituents, for by this the quantity of phosphoric acid, potash, soda and lime, &c. which the coffee draws from the soil, it must be as experience proves a very exhausting crop, and unless these materials are added to the soil in the shape of manures containing these very elements, it is impossible to get a satisfactory return in the produce.† Having considered the analysis of the plant, beans, &c. we will now turn our attention to that of the soil from which the plant was grown.

---

* Balfour's Cyclopædia of India. Supplement ii Article coffee Pages 147 and 48.

† Mr. W. H. Staines of Coonoor in a manuscript with which he kindly furnished me gives the following analysis of coffee but does not give the authority from whence derived.

Analysis.

Phosphoric acid	18·273
Sulphuric acid	0·224
Potash	15·238
Soda	6·264
Carbonate of Lime	5·828
Do. Magnesia	11·515
Chloride of Sodium	0·606
Sulphate of Lime	1·616
Phosphate of Lime	42·022
Silicic acid	0·404
	100·000

One ton of coffee removes from the soil.

	lbs.	oz.
Phosphoric acid	27·	14½
Sulphuric acid	0·	13⅓
Potash	11·	4
Soda	4·	10
Chloride of Sodium	0·	7
Lime	18.	14
Magnesia	4·	1
Silicic acid	0·	6
	68·	5

The analysis is not a quantitative determination of the several constituents entering into the composition of the soil ; that would require considerable labour, but the examination has been made more to suit the wants of planters than for publication in a scientific journal, and will I am of opinion suffice for all practical purposes. The soil was taken up from where the plant was grown, avoiding a couple of inches of the surface, as the strata for several feet below was of the same formation.

The soil has a reddish appearance, depending on the quantity of iron contained in it. It may be regarded as a sandy ferruginous loam. It does not effervesce with acids, shewing that the alkaline and earthy carbonates do not exist in it in any quantity.

1. 937 grains (2 oz. avoirdupois) dried in a dish by exposure to sun and air, lost 43·37 grains or 4·4 per cent.

2. 1 ounce of the soil was placed in a funnel, the extremity of which was loosely plugged with asbestos and 2 fluid ounces of distilled water poured over it ; the soil retained or absorbed $\frac{1}{4}$ of an ounce, or $\frac{1}{8}$ of its weight. This may be regarded as the retentive power of the soil.

3. A portion of the soil was placed in a dish and wetted with water, it formed a loosely adherent mass, and was not tough or clayey.

4. A portion of the soil was treated with water in large quantity, stirred with a rod, and the finer particles separated from the coarse by eleutriation.

The coarse particles, after being dried, were passed through a sieve to separate the sand from the gravel.

The finer particles were again treated by eleutriation to separate the clay from the sand the former being suspended in the water the latter subsiding more readily.

The soil was by the above mechanical processes separated

into 1, gravel, 2, coarse sand, 3, fine sand, and 4, into clay, which after being dried and weighed were found in the following proportions.

			Per cent.	
Gravel................	40·	0	9·	2
Coarse sand............	235·	75	53·	0
Fine sand............	30·	0	6·	8
Clay..................	138·	0	31·	0
	443·	75	100·	0

5. 1 ounce or 437·5 grains of soil were digested with 2 fluid ounces of distilled water. The water was allowed to percolate through the soil to extract soluble matter. The solution evaporated to dryness and weighed.

The residue weighed 0·1 grain, consisting of a trace of lime and organic matter.

6. The residue of the soil treated with water was digested with hydrochloric acid, and treated gently ; water was subsequently added, and the soluble parts separated from the insoluble by filtration. The hydrochloric acid solution was evaporated to dryness, redissolved in water, acidulated with hydrochloric acid to which a few drops of nitric acid were added, filtered, and tested.

There were found lime in good quantity.
Magnesia a trace.
Iron proto-per oxide in quantity.
Silica.
Alumina.
Phosphoric acid.
Potash. } Traces.
Soda. }

The hydrochloric acid dissolved in 7·12 grs. of the soil: 7·73 grs. of the dried soil were ignited in a platinum crucible to determine the quantity of organic matter, it lost 5·0 gr.,

RESULT OF THE EXAMINATION.

Gravel..................	9· 2	per cent.
Coarse sand,............	53· 0	
Fine sand...............	6· 8	
Clay....................	31· 0	
	100· 0	

Moisture 4·4 per cent.

Matter soluble in water, lime and organic matter.................... 0· 02 per cent.

Matter soluble in hydrochloric acid.

Potash and Soda traces...	0· 16 per cent.
Lime..........................	
Magnesia......................	
Aluminia......................	
Proto Sesqui oxide of iron......	
Silica........................	
Phosphoric acid	

Organic matter.................. 6·8 per cent.

I have thought it best to give the whole process in detail, as it may tend to assist planters to examine their soils if so inclined. The results will appear satisfactory, more especially when we compare it with the analysis of the ashes of the plant. In the soil will be found traces of all the ingredients requisite for the growth of the coffee plant, and it contains I may say all the ingredients essential to this particular plant, and the fruitfulness of the tree when taken up for analysis, as well as before that, was in keeping with the productive resources of the soil. We shall next turn our attention to the subject of manure.

CHAPTER V

Manure.—Coffee planters in general have not given the subject of manure the necessary attention, and by many systematic manuring is ignored altogether, from the additional expense, and in some plantations on hill sides from the difficulty in conveying manure from the bottom, attendant on their steepness. These difficulties might with a little attention to the subject be readily overcome, for manure is as essential to the plant as food to an animal; therefore to meet with not only success but a largely remunerative return, it is essential that the coffee plant be well manured, and in quantity and quality suitable to the wants of each plant, or as Dr. Wight terms it " High Farming," or in other words "*perfect tillage*" by sufficent and judicious use of manure, should be practised.

One reason why planters as a rule do not attend to manuring is, that the plantation in most instances is planted on a virgin forest land, and consequently the soil abounds with the necessary pabulum that the plant requires for the first few years of its existence, and the planter finding that the returns from his first few crops are fair, nay even handsome, and that much difficulty exists in procuring labour, or devoting the necessary time to look after manure, &c., leaving out the additional outlay, practically ignores the question, although the resources at his command are frequently ample as far as the material is concerned, if he would give the subject the necessary attention.

Having already considered the constitution of the coffee

plant, we can have no difficulty in devising suitable manures to render the speculation remunerative.

We shall now consider the different substances available as manure to the planter, and with that view divide manures into three classes, viz., Mineral, vegetable, and animal, and each of these we shall consider separately.

Mineral Manures.—There are scarcely any mineral substances available as manure in most planting localities, unless it be decaying granite, which, when well pulverized, makes a good manure for the coffee plant, from the various minerals that enter into its composition.*

Lime, where procurable, is a valuable manure, either to use occasionally as a top dressing, or to form an element in the manure, the decomposition of which it facilitates, as well as renders the manure pit less noxious than it would otherwise prove. It is also useful in decomposing and improving adhesive soils, and when properly applied, improves the land permanently, and contributes an element in the constitution of the coffee bean. When lime is not procurable, it will be found that the ashes of some trees, such as the Ashan, (*Terminalia tomentosa*) abound in lime. If the ashes of this plant be collected, mixed with water, and formed into balls, and these heated in the fire till they attain a glowing red heat, and then be hydrated with water, they will be found converted into lime; this preparation is much esteemed by the petty Rajahs in the tributary mehalls of Cuttack, and they use it with their betel instead of chunam.

Dr. Scott, late Chemical Examiner, Madras Medical College,

---

* Granite chiefly consists of quartz, feldspar, mica, and sometimes hornblende. The proportions of the 3 first are believed to be 3 feldspar, 2 quartz, and one mica. The ultimate elements of these comprise silica, alumina, potash, soda lime, magnesia, lithia, iron and manganese in small but varying quantities.

to whom I shewed some of this, analysed it, and found it to consist of the acetate-carbonate and sulphate of lime. These trees abound in all forests in India.

Vegetable Manures.—Wood ashes are valued on account of the minerals they contain,—chiefly alkalies. On looking at the analysis of the coffee plant, we see the chief ingredients that enter not only into the constitution of the plant, but that of the berries also, and we find that lime, soda, potash, phosphoric acid, &c, stand in the numerical order in which they are given, and the berries apparently require in addition phosphate and sulphate of lime and magnesia ; now most of the materials enumerated here, are found to exist in wood ashes; they are known to form a very suitable manure, and are easily procurable in this country where woods and jungles abound, and where fire is frequently had recourse to, to clear the land, and trees are obliged to be cut down. The efficacy of wood ashes consists in the large amount of saline and mineral matters that enter into its composition. Although there may be some slight difference in the quantities of the inorganic constituents of different trees, yet they will be found to have a general resemblance to each other, and therefore wood ashes will prove highly beneficial in this country, where wood ashes can be readily procured independent of burning jungle, by the daily use of wood as fuel in preparing food, &c.* "The effect of wood ashes is considerable ; besides fertilizing, they are a good substitute for lime, cheap and abundant." Some years ago, I had an analysis made of wood ashes from the jungles of Orissa, which I give here, as the wood of these jungles is much the same as that met with in coffee planting localities. The

* Liebeg says ashes of perennials, or their ingredients from any source, suffice to render the soil fertile for those plants.

quantitative analysis of this ash gave the following results, for its composition in 100 parts,

Silicious earth	30
Sulphate of lime	10
Do. muriate of soda	8
Carbonate of lime	40
Oxide of iron	4
Loss	8
	100

Charcoal.—Is invaluable as a manure. From its great absorbent power, it absorbs and retains in the soil not only moisture, but also the various volatile gases that would otherwise be dissipated. This property renders it doubly valuable, for at the same time that it holds and keeps back noxious gases, it acts as a powerful disinfectant, and if exposed to air, absorbs both air and moisture.

Jungle.—Under this term come all weeds, ferns, mosses, decaying leaves, pulp, prunings, in fact all decomposible vegetable matter, and it is these substances in a state of decay, that constitute humus or vegetable mould, and as such it is peculiarly acceptable to the coffee plant. The cost of a cwt. of jungle at most planting localities, will not exceed 8 annas to 1 rupee. All the weeds on the plantation, and those growing in the road sides and hedges, should be collected and conveyed to the dung pit, to add to the supply of manure. Fern leaves are the ordinary manure in general use; these are dried in the sun, and mixed with soil for use. The better way of preparing it for coffee plants, is to get not only ferns, but all weeds or vegetable matter procurable in the vicinity, and to put down a layer of 12 or 18 inches deep in the first instance, and then cover it over while in the green state with 6 or 8 inches of soil, and thus form a square heap of several layers thick; and to keep it in position, it might be walled round with stakes 4 or 5 feet high, and plaited with twigs and branches from the jungles, this in a little time would be sufficiently decomposed to fit it for use, and by covering in the weeds when green, none of the volatile gases will escape, and the moisture will favour or hasten its decomposition. The earth, from its absorbent power, will soak up every portion of the moisture from the green or fresh ferns, weeds, &c., and render it doubly valuable. The best kind of soil to use for the purpose will be silt from adjacent swamps, tanks, nullahs, and rivulets ; this should be carefully taken up to the extent of 8 or 12 inches in depth annually, and laid while fresh or moist over the vegetable matter, and any kind of common soil laid on this to the extent of an inch or two, will answer extremely well.

Many planters, after getting in a crop, do not seem to care about the shells of the coffee ; when the beans are freed from the fruit in the dried state, or even pulped fresh in the cherry state, these are frequently wasted or thrown away. This is a great mistake, for every thing belonging to the plant, from the washings of the bean, pulp, skins, of the berries recent or dry, is an addition to the manure pits. Advantage should be taken of the return of the coolies for their meals at noon, and their return home in the evening ; they should be made to take a basket of the pulp or shells, or a pot or bucket of the washings, and on their way deposit it in the manure pit. The washings will be readily absorbed by the contents of the pit, and will tend to favour decomposition the more readily. This system will greatly enrich the contents of the pit. Even if spirits have been distilled, the refuse of the still should be conveyed to the manure pit, for most of the elements necessary for the plant will still be found to exist in the refuse.

Some are in the habit of throwing the dried shells into the cow-house, where from their dry state they readily absorb the urine, &c., and are subsequently removed to the manure pit.

Oil Cake Poonac.—Is useful as a manure, the following kinds are available :—

Cake from Gingilie seeds (*Sesamun Orientale*) ; Eloopai (*Bassia longifolia*) castor oil or (*Ricinis Communis*) lamp oil or (*Ricinus Communis fructibus majoribus*) Mustard (*Sinapis nigra*) cotton (*Gossypium*) neem (*Azadirachta Indica*) pinna kai (*Calophyllum Inophyllum*). All these oil cakes possess more or less the same properties ; that of the gingilie seed is in general use for cattle as food, but in most places it can be purchased at from 3 to 6 Rs. the cwt. ; most of the other varieties are frequently used as fuel or thrown on the dung heap, and may be got for the asking, or at best may be purchased at from 1 to 2 Rs. the cwt. The cake of the elloopai is used instead of soap as a detergent to cleanse the skin, but may be purchased for a mere trifle.

These several oil cakes chiefly consist of water, oil, sugar, aluminous compounds, and ash ; and the ultimate elements of the ash comprise silica, phosphates, and free phosphoric acid, all of which are invaluable to the coffee plant.

Animal Manures.—Farm yard manure. By this term is meant the dung and urine of cattle, goats, &c., with the refuse litter or straw, &c. These should be carefully preserved and used as manure. On some estates a large number of cattle are kept. In such cases their dung and urine should be carefully preserved. In the building of byres or cow sheds, the two sides of the building should be raised, well metalled, and sloped down to the centre into a deepish groove, leading on one side of the building into a large pit for the reception of the urine, and the ground sprinkled with straw or litter, weeds, such as ferns, mosses, &c., to absorb the moisture of the byre. Pigeon and poultry dung, and the contents of pig styes are valuable as manure. Each plantation should have its pigeon cote, poultry yard, and piggery. If these are properly managed, not only will the planter's table be supplied with delicacies in the way of young pigeons, chickens, eggs, bacon, &c., but the plantation will derive great benefit from the manure. A two storied house, the upper room for pigeons and the lower for rabbits, should be built on all plantations, and the pigeon house, if managed with care, will soon become a refuge for wild, or blue pigeons, and these, while they seek their own food, will give the planter a good supply of dung. As for rabbits, the vicinity of every plantation will furnish them with abundance of green food, by which they may be kept in the best condition. Pigeons, poultry, and rabbit's dung stand in the order here given and form excellent manures, more especially on coffee estates, where they supply the planter with meat as well as his plantation with manure. The following analysis of pigeon's and poultry dung, is taken from M. Girardin's work on manures.

	Fresh dung of pigeons.	Fresh dung of poultry.
Water	79· 00	72· 90
Organic matter acting as manure	18· 11	16· 20
Saline matter acting as a stimulant	2· 28	5· 24
Gravel / Silicious sand	0· 61	5· 66
	100· 00	100· 00*

* Des Fumiers considérés comme engrais par J. Girardin Paris 1847.

I am not aware of rabbits dung having been analysed, but "it has been used as a manure with great success by Mr. Fane who finds it profitable to keep rabbits in such a manner as to preserve their dung."*

Urine of all animals is extremely valuable as manure. It contains large quantities of the essential elements of vegetables, requisite for the well being and health of plants in a state of solution. But it should be remembered that urine readily decomposes by a putrefactive process, and therefore if not used mixed up with solid manure, it may with advantage be used in its recent state, diluted with water. The species of urine that contain most albumen, gelatine and urea, are the best as manures. The following table, giving the constituents of the different kinds of urine, is taken from the table of analysis, comparative values and equivalents of manure, (Translated from the French of M. M. Boussingault and Payen).†

---

* Agricultural Chemistry by Davy and Shier 1844, Page 237.

† Vide Davy and Shier's Agricultural Chemistry 1844—Pages 247, 48, 49, and 50.

TABLE OF THE ANALYSIS, COMPARATIVE VALUES, AND EQUIVALENTS OF MANURES.

Names of Substances.	Normal water.	Nitrogen in 100 parts of the substance dried.	Nitrogen in 100 parts of the substance in its normal state	Values.		Equivalents.		REMARKS.
				Substance dried.	Substance in its normal state.	Substance dried	Substance in its normal state.	
Farm yard manure... ...	79·3	1·95	0·40	100·	100·	100.	100·	
Solid Excrement of cows.	85·9	2·30	0·32	117·9	80·	84·78	12· 5	
Do. of horses.........	75·3	2·21	0·55	113·3	137·5	88· 2	72· 7	
Urine of cows...	88·3	3·80	0·44	194·9	110·	51· 3	90· 9	
Do. of horses...........	79·1	12·50	2·61	641·	652·5	15· 6	15· 3	The Horse drank very little [urine very thick.
Mixed excrement of cows...............	84·3	2·59	0·41	132·8	102·5	75·28	97·56	Result calculated.
Do. of horses..........	75·4	30· 2	0·74	156·9	185·	64·56	54·	
Excrement of swine......	81·4	3·37	0·63	172·8	157·5	57·86	63· 4	
,, sheep	63·0	2·99	1·11	153·3	277·5	65· 2	36·	
,, goats......	46·0	3·93	2·16	201·5	540·	49· 6	18· 5	
Pigeon's dung......	9·6	9·02	8·30	462·6	207·5	21· 4	4· 8	From Bechelbronn.
Urine of the Public Urinals...	9·57	17·566	16·853	900·3	4213·25	11· 1	2·37	Dried in the Stove.
Do. do.	96·889	33·108	0·715	118·5	178·8	8· 4	55·94	Ammonia included.

Night Soil—Is a most valuable and powerful manure, if properly applied.

The number of coolies on a plantation should be taken advantage of, and proper places prepared on different parts of the estate, and to any one of these they should be directed to go, when requiring to relieve themselves ; although it differs in composition from some of the others enumerated here, and is extremely liable to decompose, it contains a large amount of carbon, hydrogen, nitrogen and oxygen, all of which are essentially necessary for the coffee plant, and in whatever state applied either fresh or decomposed it supplies food for plants in abundance ; quick lime or charcoal will readily destroy any bad smell that may arise from it or a layer of fresh soil one inch thick will be found sufficient not only to absorb and retain the gaseous matter but also to remove all offensive smell.

Liebeg* gives the following ultimate analysis of fæces (night soil) by Playfair.

Carbon	45· 24
Hydrogen	6· 88
Nitrogen-Oxygen	34· 73
Ashes	13· 15
	100· 00
Water	300· 00
	400·

* Animal Chemistry 2nd Ed. P. 285.

Berzilius gives*

Water	73·3
Albumen	0·9
Bile	0·9
Mucilage, fat and other animal matters	16·7
Saline matter	1·2
Undecomposed food	7·0
	100·00

According to Playfair, 5½ ounces of fæces are allowed daily to each Soldier on an average; they contain 75 per cent. of water, and the dry residue contains 45·24 per cent. of carbon, and 13·15 per cent. of ashes. But if we make allowance for the vegetable diet of coolies, and even take it at one-half the quantity given here, we can see at once the advantage gained by a number of coolies; for instance, if we start at 50, we shall have 9 lbs. of night soil daily added to the dung pit.

My experiments in the jail at Chingleput, give on an average 3 oz. of fæces daily to each Prisoner.

Bones.—Prove valuable in consequence of the large amount of phosphate of lime they contain, and from the analysis of the coffee bean it will be seen that this forms one of the most essential ingredients that enter into its composition, but the planter seldom has the means at command, to enable him to take advantage of this substance as manure. In order to render it effective, it will have to be crushed first, and then digested with sulphuric acid. To do the former, a crushing mill of some simple construction is necessary, and in the use of the latter much care will be required. It must not be entrusted to any but intelligent hands, to prevent accidents; these are risks in which planters do not like to involve themselves. Sulphuric acid is manufactured by Messrs. Barrie and Co. at Madras, from whom it can be procured in any quantity at 4 annas per lb.

* Animal Chemistry 2nd Ed. P. 285.

The acid can be sent to any part of the country, and is usually put into green stoppered bottles, well secured with dammer and straw ropes.

Bones, according to Berzilius, contain 55 per cent. of the phosphates of lime and magnesia. But bones will be found to differ very materially in their constituents, according to the different animals from which they are taken. According to the analysis of Fourcroy and Vauquelin, ox bones are composed of

Decomposable animal matter	51·	0
Phosphate of lime	37·	7
Carbonate of lime	10·	0
Phosphate of magnesia	1·	3
	*100.	0

M. Merat Guillot has given the following estimate of the composition of the bones of different animals. The bones of old animals are proportionately more valuable than those of young ones, as in the former the quantity of earthy matter is greater, which renders them brittle, while the young owe their toughness to the greater quantity of animal matter.

Animals.	Phosphate of lime.	Carbonate of lime.
Bone of Calf	54·	
„ Horse	67·5	1·25
„ Sheep	70·	5·
„ Elk	90·	1·
„ Hog	52·	1·
„ Pullet	72·	1·5
„ Hare	85·	1·
„ Pike	64·	1·
„ Carp	45·	5·
Horses' teeth	85·5	2·5
Ivory	64·	1·
Hartshorn	27·	1·

*Davy and Shiers Agricultural Chemistry 1844. Pages 224 and 25.

The remaining parts of the hundred must be considered as decomposable animal matter. Human bones, according to Marchand and Berzilius, consist of :

Cartilage insoluble in muriatic acid......	27·	23
Soluble in „ „	5·	02
Vessels...........................	1·	01
Basic phosphate of lime................	52·	26
Fluoride of calcium....................	1·	00
Carbonate of lime......................	10·	21
Phosphate of magnesia..............	1·	05
Soda................................	0·	92
Chloride of Sodium....................	0·	25
Oxides of iron and manganese, and loss..	1·	5
	* 100·	00

Thus it will be seen at a glance how essential the constituents of bone are to the coffee plant. That phosphates are of the greatest importance to coffee will become apparent at once, for they enter not only into the composition of the coffee bean, but into the seeds of most plants, and as a manure their fertilizing influence is perennial.

Bones are readily had for the trouble of collecting, and the more so as they are not sought after in India to undergo the process of boiling, which they do in England on account of the grease they contain, and any expense in pulverizing them will be made up by the increase of fertilizing power they give to the plant. Grinding, crushing, and burning, are the usual modes, but to render these more largely productive, Professor Von Liebeg recommends the use of sulphuric acid.—" Pour over crushed bones or bone ashes half their weight of sulphuric acid, diluted with four parts

* Davy and Shiers Agricultural Chemistry 1841. Pages 221 and 25.

of water, and digest for 24 hours, add one hundred parts of water."* But the inconvenience of carriage, the necessary apparatus, and the want of intelligent workmen to carry out this process, render it difficult of being put into practice saving in exceptional cases. " The effect of bones unless fresh, is said to be more in fruit than foliage. Half a measure to each tree, gives an increase of 2 cwt. per acre for 6 years." " Yellow leaves and black berries are quite restored by bones."† Although bones digested with sulphuric acid form an extremely valuable manure, yet as its manufacture would be attended with much labour and expense to the planter, it is necessary that advantage should be taken of such substances as are in his immediate vicinity, and which will probably prove equally valuable.

Animal charcoal when procurable, is as valuable as vegetable, and might with advantage be brought into use in the manufacture of manure ; nay all animal substances, from the putrid carcase to the dung, are exceedingly valuable.

Manure Pit.—The pit should be excavated in proportion to the wants of the estate, and the bottom and sides should either be metalled or faced with stones, or what is better, built pucka into a cistern and covered with thatch. Into this pit not only the dung and urine from the byres, but the contents of privies and latrines should be emptied ; all vegetable and animal refuse, washings of meat, fish, &c., weeds, decaying wood, refuse from the pulp house, &c., should be thrown in here, and once a week either a fine layer of charcoal or some quick lime must be dusted over and a layer of about one inch of soil spread over all ; by following this system the pit will be completely deodorised and at the same time decomposition facilitated, and in a few months a valuable supply of manure rich in fertilizing pro-

---

* Davy and Shiers Agricultural Chemistry 1844. Page 224.

† Mr. Staines Memoranda.

perties, and containing all the elements necessary for the coffee plant in particular, will be procured. Where plantations are situated on hill sides, secondary dung pits should exist at different heights, and the coolies compelled to resort here to relieve themselves, and weeds, prunings, and other available rubbish should be deposited here to form manure. By adopting this system, the expense of conveying manure from the bottom to the top will be to a great extent avoided.

If it is necessary to prepare manure on the spot, the best kind may at once be manufactured, by mixing equal parts of wood ashes and rotten farm yard manure, to which if procurable a 20th part of pigeon's or poultry dung may be added. This manure can always be prepared on the spot, and will be found on analysis to carry all the elements necessary for the nourishment of the coffee plant. Lime when procurable should be added in small quantities. Mr. Staines, in his valuable memoranda, gives Perindorge's receipt for manure, but the authority from whence procured is not given, nevertheless I cannot do better than copy it in here.

Instructions for preparing a heap of 2,100 cubic feet, or about 40 tons.

" In any convenient part of the estate, and near a small supply of water if possible, erect with jungle posts, a kraal or pen 30 feet long, 10 feet wide, and 7 high. This may easily be done, by digging a trench 2 feet deep around a space of ground of those dimensions, setting the posts closely side by side, and pounding in the clay well about their feet."

" The posts do not require tying, as they are merely intended as walls to retain the heap of manure for a short time. A light and temporary roof of branches is also desirable, to keep off the sun and part of the heaviest rain that might wash through the heap."

" The bottom or floor of the kraal ought to be sunk a foot or two lower than the surrounding ground, to prevent the escape of the liquid manure."

" Commence making the compost, by spreading on the floor of the pen a layer about 18 inches thick of fresh weeds, grasses, leaves, small succulent branches, or in fact any kind of green vegetable matter. If the vegetable matter, of whatever sort, be long, it ought to be chopped, for the purpose of facilitating the removal and application of the manure afterwards. At the same time put a layer of earth next the posts, to prevent drainage at the sides ; but on the second occasion of using the kraal, this edge stratum may be conveniently formed of a little of the manure that was previously made."

" Over the 18 inch layer of weeds, &c., spread some cattle manure—the more, of course the better—but a few inches—say 6—will be sufficient."

" Then pour over the heap as equally as possible, a portion—say one-sixth part—of Pickle No. 1, well stirred up before use. The same process is to be pursued daily until the pen is filled somewhat above the tops of the posts. Nothing more should then be done for a week, with the exception of taking care to keep the heap moist by sprinkling water over it occasionally, or even daily if necessary, in hot weather."

" At the end of a week make holes with a long crowbar down through the heap, about one foot apart and funnel shaped at the top, to within 18 inches of the bottom, and pour into them one-third of Pickle No. 2. Next day make other holes between those first made, and to within 3 feet of the bottom, and pour in the same quantity of Pickle No. 2. On the third day make the holes to about 5 feet from the bottom, and pour in the remainder of the pickle. Then cover over with old manure or soil, and in a week or ten days the compost will be fit for application."

Pickle No. 1.—Put 2 bushels of bone dust, 1 bushel of wood ashes, and about a quart of fresh burnt lime, to steep for a few days in as much water as will cover them. Then throw them into a mixture of 20 gallons of ferment, and 300 gallons of water. Add a bushel of lime, and mix all well together. Stir them up also when taking out part to apply.

Note.—The object of macerating the bone dust in potash and lime, is to remove the oil which prevents bone from speedily decomposing. The oil is thus converted into soap; and the plant is then enabled to make use of the phosphate of lime contained in the bone. This pickle can be made in smaller quantities for convenience: a couple of Beer casks would hold 50 gallons or a sixth part of the above—that is sufficient for a day's consumption in making 40 tons of manure.

The "Ferment."—Take 5 gallons of molasses, 15 gallons of water (warm is preferable), mix in a Beer cask or other suitable vessel, and keep in a close warm room for a couple of days, when it will be fit for use. This will be ascertained by a scum or froth rising on the surface. If molasses are not procurable, common coarse sugar or jaggery may be substituted, in the proportion of 8 lbs. to every gallon of molasses.

Note.—The Ferment is most required on cold high estates.

Pickle No. 2.—Sal-ammoniac 20lbs., common salt 20lbs., 10 gallons of ferment, filled to 300 gallons of water: 20 lbs. of saltpetre may be added if easily procurable, but it may be omitted with very little detriment. Add any fresh cattle manure that is to be had.

Note.—The salts should be thoroughly dissolved in a sufficient quantity of the water, before mixing them with the other ingredients.

Remarks.—Thus in about 20 or 25 days from the commencement of operations, there will be made a heap of most valuable manure, which ought to be sufficient for four acres of coffee at the rate of ½ bushel for each tree, but of course the quantity must depend upon the more or less exhausted condition of the soil. The object of the above process, is in the first place to hasten decay in the vegetable matter, by artificially exciting fermentation, and the chemical changes dependant upon that action. This effected, the other materials which the vegetable matter does not possess in sufficient quantity for the coffee tree, are then added, and in a manner that prevents their dissipation or loss. The whole mass is thus brought into the condition most suitable for being taken up by the roots of the trees. Cattle manure is of course the best form under which nutriment can be furnished, to most fruit bearing trees ; and the compost as above made is a tolerably close imitation of cattle manure. It must be borne in mind, that cattle discharge no materials as manure—either in excrement or urine, which they have not previously taken in with their food. The vegetable matter which forms the basis of this artificial manure being, however, equal in quality to what cattle generally consume, and being rather deficient, although not altogether wanting in some materials; these are added in a manner not only most economical, but also calculated to preserve them from loss. The cattle manure used is intended not only for its own inherent value, but for assisting by a well-known chemical law, the assimilation of the other materials to the same condition as itself. A few cattle will sufficiently answer this purpose, although the amount of their manure if used alone would be of little avail. The cow is a small natural laboratory, in which chemical changes are continually going on, and the heap above described is for the purposes of manure, making an artificial imitation of the cow on a large scale. Rather it should be said the heap closely resembles so much farm yard manure—that is consists of a supply of carbonacious matter, in the condition most suitable for supplying the plants with this prime necessary; with the salts (both of excrement and urine) universally, equally and in sufficient quantity diffused throughout the mass."

If the necessary attention be paid to the particular kind of manure after the manner detailed here, it will be found rich in fertilizing properties, and a pound or two annually will add more to the productiveness of the plant, than whole baskets of the rubbish I have sometimes seen used under the name of manure.

In the use of manure, care should be taken that it is not allowed to be exposed for any length of time, by which the essential ingredients will be volatilised, and thus the most valuable part of it be lost, but the plants should be dug round from the depth of from 4 to 6 inches previously, and as soon as the manure reaches the plant, it should be laid down and immediately covered over with the soil. If care be exercised in the disposition of coolies, this will be found as feasible as any other system in vogue.

The manure from the pit should have rotted thoroughly before it is taken up, for if used whilst in a state of fermentation, it frequently kills the plants or proves otherwise injurious to the roots.

The manuring will only have to be carried out once a year, as soon as the crop has been taken off the plants, and should be commenced immediately before or after handling and pruning.

In digging up the soil about the roots of plants, it is a good plan to remove all superficial roots that are attached to the root stems, to the extent of some 4 or 6 inches according to circumstances, for these roots will be found useless; instead of drawing nourishment from the soil for the support of the plant, their absorbing vessels will be found clogged up with woody matter, and the nutriment taken up by the more active rootlets be diverted for their own nourishment, and thus deprive the plant of its proper supply, acting the part of so much useless wood, and a mere burden to the plant. In their removal they should be cut close to the stem, without injuring the root stem itself. This will enable the plant to throw out fresh rootlets, which will prove much more active in the absorption of nourishment from the soil, and add to the increase and vigour of the plant itself, and render it much more prolific.

In the application of manure some care will be necessary, but it is a mistake to apply the manure to the root stem, for it is not the base of the roots that take up nourishment, but it is the extremities of the roots where the spongioles are situated, and they move from the stem in search of soil to feed upon, so that in the deposition of manure it should be placed from, 8 to 24 inches from the stem, according to the age of the plant. In some instances double that distance may be necessary, for in good soil the roots will be found to expand equally with the crown of the plant. With reference to plants situated on the slopes of high ground or on steep hill sides, the opening around the soil for the reception of manure should be a semi-circle on the highest part, and if the manure be deposited here, as moisture is absorbed, its elements will spread to the lower part of the soil, and thus bring it within the reach of every part of the roots of the plant.

CHAPTER VI.

Cost of Planting, &c.—Capitalists and speculators in coffee planting are generally anxious to know particulars, with reference to the amount of capital required for an undertaking of the kind, and the details of operation as to particular items with reference to planting, to enable them to understand the matter thoroughly before investing their money in coffee planting. Such information at best is difficult of attainment, for the different localities in India where coffee may be successfully cultivated differ so very much, not only with reference to soil and climate, but also as regards the command of labour, the kind of land whether forest, bamboo, jungle, or otherwise, all these will have to be taken into account,* nevertheless : allowing for such contingencies, we cannot go far wrong in laying down a scale to guide the planter in his operations.

The cost of opening 200 acres of forest land for the cultivation of coffee, including purchase of land, tools, felling, clearing, lining, holing, filling holes, planting, road making, building cottage, maistry's hut, coolies lines, &c., and keeping the same in order for the first three years after the date on which the forest commences to be felled, is as follows :

---

* Some localities are subject to the N. E. rather than to the S. W. monsoon, whilst others suffer from both, and others from neither; these are points that should be remembered.

First Year.	Rs.	A.	P.
Value of land at 5 Rs. per acre............	1,000	0	0
Felling jungle at 10 Rs. per acre............	2,000	0	0
Clearing, burning, &c.	100	0	0
Lining and marking out pits................	300	0	0
Holing or excavation of pits................	1,000	0	0
Filling in holes..........................	300	0	0
Planting................................	300	0	0
Nurseries...............................	600	0	0
Native supervision........................	360	0	0
European supervision at 100 Rs. per month...	1,200	0	0
Total Rs...	7,160	0	0

Second Year.	Rs.	A.	P.
12 monthly weedings.......................	800	0	0
Suppling failures.........................	100	0	0
Nurseries...............................	300	0	0
Monsooning roads.........................	100	0	0
Handling trees...........................	100	0	0
Thatching and repairing cottage and coolies lines	100	0	0
Native supervision........................	360	0	0
European supervision at 120 per month........	1,440	0	0
Total Rs..	3,300	0	0

Third Year.	Rs.	A.	P.
12 monthly weedings.......................	800	0	0
Supplying failures........................	200	0	0
Nurseries...............................	300	0	0
Monsooning roads.........................	100	0	0
Handling and pruning......................	200	0	0
Thatching and repairing cottage lines, &c.....	100	0	0
Picking crop.............................	500	0	0
Native supervision........................	360	0	0
European supervision at 150 Rs. per month....	1,800	0	0
Contingencies............................	100	0	0
Total Rs...	4,460	0	0

Instruments, &c.	Rs.	A.	P.
Axes 150	200	0	0
Mamoties 150	200	0	0
Crowbars 150	150	0	0
Cutties 50*	50	0	0
Pickaxes 30	50	0	0
Pruning knives	50	0	0
Total Rs.	700	0	0

Buildings, Roads, &c.

Superintendent's cottage	1,000	0	0
Head maistry's hut	30	0	0
Coolies lines	200	0	0
Road making	500	0	0
Contingencies	100	0	0
Total Rs.	1,830	0	0

Thus the total cost of a plantation for three years will be as follows :—

First year	7,160	0	0
Second year	3,300	0	0
Third year	4,460	0	0
Instruments, &c	700	0	0
Buildings, Roads, &c	1,830	0	0
Total Rs.	17,450	0	0

The outlay will then be 17,450 Rs. for the three years.†

The third year is supposed to make a return. The average produce of an acre is estimated at 7 cwt. but we

* A kind of chopper or bill hook.

† This estimate is applicable to Coorg and Wynad more particularly the former.

could not do better than keep on the safe side and take the produce of an acre at 5 cwt. The 200 acres will yield 1,000 cwt. of coffee beans, and if we take the value of a cwt. at 28 Rs. (that is giving 7 Rs. to the maund of 25 lbs.), the return will be 18,000 Rs., giving a return of cent. per cent. After the third year, the annual expense will not exceed 5,000 Rs. on a well managed plantation, and the profit subsequently will be something fabulous.

But as already intimated, the success will depend on a proper selection of locality, choice of site, and other favorable contingencies, but at the same time one should bear in mind that in some seasons a complete failure may take place, whilst in others double the estimated produce may be obtained; for from 10 to 15 cwt. per acre has been produced on some estates, and like all mercantile transactions, the larger the scale on which planting is conducted, so in proportion will the expense decrease and the return increase. I here give a second estimate intended for the Wynaad, which was drawn up by a friend for 150 acres, and is considered rather a low estimate.

	Rs.	A.	P.
Land	2,000	0	0
Felling at 7 Rs. per acre	1,050	0	0
Nurseries	500	0	0
Lining	80	0	0
Holing at 9 Rs. per acre	1,350	0	0
Planting	75	0	0
Roads	200	0	0
Lines and house	200	0	0
Tools, 50 axes at 1¼ each, and 50 mamooties at 1¼ each	112	8	0
25 cutties at 1 R. each, and 25 crowbars at 1¼ R. each	56	4	0
Sundries	200	0	0
Superintendent for first year at 100 Rs.	1,200	0	0
Maistries 30 Rs. per month	360	0	0
Weeding for 1st year	200	0	0
Total Rs.	7,583	8	0

This is for one year, and taken at an average, we may safely put it down at 20,000 Rs. for the 3 years, for 150 acres, and then we shall not lose much either way. Both these estimates may be made applicable to any of the coffee growing localities in India, with safety.

In neither of these estimates have I made allowances for pulping and otherwise preparing the coffee berry for the market: these will at best form but a small item. It is the belief that speculation in coffee makes a return of cent. per cent., that has drawn out so many speculators in this line; and unfortunately small capitalists who embark in the speculation, when they find their means exhausted, allow their estates to run wild, and at the same time expect to realize their expectations, in which they are usually disappointed. A few give it up in disgust, and others give their estates as little care as possible, and endeavour to draw from them as much as they will produce in their uncultivated state.

The grand mistake made by planters, is in the indiscriminate cutting down of forest. Trees whose shade was necessary for the protection of the plant against the scorching heat of the sun, are cut down, and streams in their vicinity allowed to run dry, depriving the plants at the same time of shade and moisture.

It should be remembered that although the climate in most of the coffee growing localities is mild, the sun's rays are powerful, and tell with scorching effect on the young leaves and tender shoots of the coffee plant. Under these circumstances, we are not surprised to find those plants in coffee plantations which are in exposed situations, neither protected by hill sides, nor by the shade of trees, looking yellow and stunted, from being deprived of the moisture necessary for their vigorous growth.

Whilst on this subject, I cannot do better than give here a calculation drawn up by the "Neilgherry and Mysore Coffee and Tea Company," as it appeared in the local journals, in an account of an action before the court of Queen's Bench, London, the other day, shewing the cost of coffee cultivation for one acre.

"Cost of land and planting with two year old trees, 850 to the acre.

	£.	s.	d.
Weeding, second year	12	0	0
Third year, &c................	4	0	0
Total....	16	0	0

The produce of the 4th year, at 8 cwt. per acre, at 80s. per cwt., £32 0 0, which after all deductions is estimated to leave at least a profit of 16 £ per acre; and for the fifth and sixth years, the average produce is on a most moderate estimate 12 cwt. per acre, or even higher."

Another company, the "Colonial Coffee Company," under the provision of the limited liability act, gives the following detailed estimate for purchasing 3,000 acres of forest land in Ceylon. It is taken from the "*Overland Ceylon Times*" for October 1860. I give the whole estimate as therein detailed, as it contains much valuable information on the subject.

Detailed estimate for purchasing 3,000 acres of forest land in Ceylon.

Planting 2,000 thereof with coffee and bringing the same into bearing, including all cost of the necessary buildings and all other expenses.

Proposed capital £50,000. Purchasing in July 1860 of 3,000 acres, at say £2 per acre beyond the upset price of £1 per acre, and survey fees £9,500.

Estate and carpenter's, &c., tools £500.

Felling and clearing No. 1 lot of 500 acres, £1,000.

Nurseries for young plants and stumps, £200.

Lining and planting (dibbling) at 12s. per acre, £300.

Connecting land with main road, &c., £300.

Labourer's residences £200.

Expenses of sending to India to secure labourers, £100.

Superintendent's salary for 9 months, at £50 per month, £450.

One mill wright and field assistant superintendent, half year £200.

One office and field assistant superintendent, half year £100.

Passage money of the same to Ceylon, £200.

One permanent bungalow £200.

Weeding 500 acres, for 3 months, £200.

London expenses; viz. cost of direction, Secretary and offices, £1,250.

Colombo expenses £500.

Remitting £14,000 at 20s. per cent., freight, insurance, &c., £280.

Contingencies 10 per cent. on above outlay, £1,568.

First year's (1860) expenditure, £ 16,948.

1861—Up-keep of 500 acres.

Weeding £400.

Roads extension and repair, £200.

Superintendents and assistants salaries, £1,200.

London expenses £1,250.

Colombo do. £700.

Felling and clearing Lot No. 2, 500 acres £1,000.

Nurseries and stumps £150.

Lining and planting £300.

Weeding £200.

Roads £100.

Permanent lines £250.

Do. pulping house machinery £700.

Do. stores £700.

Do. bungalow £400.

Remitting £6,000—£120.

Contingencies on £7,970, at 10 per cent., £797.

Expenses of 1861, second year, £8,467.

1862—Up-keep of lots No. 1 and 2, 1,000 acres.

Weeding £750.

Handling £200.

Supplying vacancies £150.

Roads extending and repairing £250.

Superintendent's and assistant's salaries, £1,200.

Tools £150.

London and Colombo expenses, £1,950.

Felling, &c., No. 3, 500 acres, £1,000.

Nurseries and stumps £150.

Lining and planting, £300.

Permanent Lines £200.

Tools £50.

Roads connecting and extending, £350.

Bungalow for assistant £150.

Field assistant's salary £200.

Remitting £6,000 at 2 per cent. £120.

Crop expenses on 2,000 cwts. the produce of No. 1, planted in November 1860.

Picking and curing, at 7s. per cwt. £700.

Transport to seaport, £500.

Bags, &c. £400.

Expenses of 1862 (3rd year), £8,783.

1863—Up-keep of 1,500 acres ; viz. Weeding £1,000—Handling 750£. Converting bridle into cart roads, £200.

Two sets of work as above, £1,300.

Tools £200.

Permanent lines £300.

Supplying failures £250.

Superintendent's Salary £700.

Three Assistants £1,000.

London and Colombo expenses, £2,050—£7,950.

Medical sub-assistants, for medical supervision of coolies, salary and medicines, £300.

Opening No. 4 lot of 500 acres, £2,000.

Crop expenses on 3,500 cwt. from No. 1.

Ditto on 2,000 do. from No. 2, 5,500 cwt. at 16s. per cwt. at seaport, £4,400.

Exchange on remitting, £13,000 £650.

Contingencies 10 per cent. on £16,000—£1,600.

Expenses incurred to date in erecting a curing establishment, £1,000.

Expenses of 1863 (4th year) £17,900.

1864. Estimate of expenditure.

Crop, 16,000 cwt.

Superintendent's salary £800.

Millwright assistants do. £400.

Four field assistants and a clerk, £800.

Weeding 2,000 acres, at 18s.—£1,800.

Handling £1,800.

Cross draining £500.

Completing roads £800.

Third set of works £1,300.

Additional lines and up-keep £200.

Addition to up-keep of works £400.

Principal Bungalow £600.

Picking and curing 16,000 cwt., at 6s.—£8,800.

Transport of crop, £4,000.

Bags, &c. &c. £500.

Cattle Establishment £1,000.

Immigration tax £200.

Manuring £500.

Medical and contingent charges, £900.

Money charges (exchange) £1,100.

London and Colombo expenses, £2,050.

16,000 cwt. at 30s. Expenses of 1864 (5th year) £24,450.

1865—Estimate of expenditure, crop 18,000 cwts.

Superintendent's salary £1,000.

Millwright assistant's do. £1,000.

Four field assistants £1,000. Clerk £100. Weeding £1,800.

Handling £1,800.

Opening 300 acres, £1,200.

Tools and machinery £400.

Cattle Establishment £1,000.

Picking and curing, at 6s., £5,400.

Transport at 5s., £4,000.

Draining, £1,000.

Roads £700.

Addition to and up-keep of buildings, £1,000.

London and Colombo expenses, £2,200.

Bags, &c. £500.

Manuring £1,000.

Immigration tax £300.

Medical and contingent charges, £700.

Money charges, £1,200.

18,000 cwts. at 80s. Expenses of 1865 (6th year) £27,200.

Total expenses to 31st December 1865 £103,548.

Position as per account current (A) 31st December 1865.

" Valuation."

2,000 acres of land in full bearing, with all the buildings, roads, cattle establishments, complete, from which an annual crop of 18,000 cwts. can be relied upon, and produced at a cost of 25s. per cent. at the port of shipment; and at that rate the property would be kept in thorough repair and condition, capable of producing such average crop for an indefinite number of years,—and allowing the average price of coffee in London to be only 65s. per cwt., there would be an annual profit of 25s. on 18,000 cwt., which at 5 year's purchase, the market price of estates in Ceylon, would amount to..........................£112,500 0 0

There would also be 300 acres of young coffee, worth say £15 per acre.................. „	4,500 0 0
And as current expenditure in the curing establishment (if such is approved of) may be charged to "Preparation," the original outlay, independent of improved value, may be accepted.... ....„	1,000 0 0
Total value of properties........	£1,18,000 0 0
Annual income say............	£ 20,000 0 0

ACCOUNT CURRENT.

Dr.

Dec. 1862—To Nett value at the port of shipment of 2,000 cwt..................	£	5,000
„ 1863—To do. 5,500 cwt............	„	13,750
„ 1864—To do. 16,000 cwt............	„	40,000
„ 1865—To do. 18,000 cwt............	„	45,000
	£	103,750

Cr.

Dec. 1860—By capital......................	£	16,948
„ 1861— „ „	„	8,467
„ 1862— „ and acceptances........... ...	„	8,783
„ 1863— „ „	„	17,900
„ 1864— „ „	„	24,450
„ 1865— „ „	„	27,200
Balance without interest....................	„	2
	£	103,750

I am indebted to W. H. Staines, Esq., of Coonoor, for the following particulars about that locality. "The cost of land has risen from 5 Rs. to 15 or 20 the acre; most of the other operations are carried on at contract rates. For instance, felling 18 Rs. the acre, holing and lining 18 Rs., weeding one rupee monthly. Picking crop, at 30 Rs. per ton. Every 50 coolies have lines built for them, chiefly of mud and thatch: no head maistries' huts. The best building on the estate is of brick and tiles—allowances made and space left for roads, which are only carried out as the plantation succeeds. These differ from a footpath to a cart road. The natives, when employed as maistries' get from 6 to 9 rupees. Superintendents from 15 to 20 Rs., Europeans 50 Rs. a month.

The value of machinery varies from that of a 25£ pulper to that of a 100£, with water wheel and other expensive adjuncts. Two hundred rupees will purchase nearly all the instruments required on the estate.

Monsooning roads is a term unknown in that country, as the monsoon is by no means heavy. As to handling and pruning, there is no rule; while some prune severely, others moderately, others slightly, some do not prune at all, and if planting is rightly carried out, there should be few failures to supply."

Although it is generally believed that the planter will realize his return on the 3rd or 4th year, allowances are never made for a year lost in making the start; such as securing land, looking about, getting up a nursery, or securing plants to purchase, collecting coolies, &c., so that a year is generally lost in arranging these preliminaries; consequently 5 years should be taken into account to get a return, but as far as the actual operation of planting is concerned, the return is procurable on the 3rd or 4th year, provided the planter is in a position to start at once which happens very rarely indeed.

For the following estimate on the Shervaroys, I am indebted to B. A. Daly, Esq., a gentleman who has spent some 22 years of his life in planting operations. This estimate is for grass land. Cost of a plantation of 100,000 tress, planted six feet apart on grass land.

1st Year.

	Rs.	A.	P.
Nursery for planting out	100	0	0
Purchase of land, 100 acres at 5 Rs. per acre	500	0	0
Cattle 100 heads, at 10 Rs. per head	1,000	0	0
Cattle shed	150	0	0
Cooly lines	200	0	0
Manure pit	50	0	0
Tools and a cart for use	250	0	0
Clearing jungle	200	0	0
To 100,000 pits, at 12¼ Rs. per 1,000	1,225	0	0
Planting	100	0	0
Attending to the plants, the first year after planting	100	0	0
To four maistry's wages, at 7 Rs. each per month	336	0	0
Wages of three cow-boys	180	0	0
Rs.	4,391	0	0

2nd Year.

	Rs.	A.	P.
To trenching land planted	4,000	0	0
To manuring	1,000	0	0
To cow-boy's wages	180	0	0
To maistry's wages	336	0	0
To fern & other materials for making manure.	200	0	0
Rs.	5,716	0	0

3rd Year.

	Rs.	A.	P.
To three hoeings..............................	3,000	0	0
To manuring..............................	1,000	0	0
To cow-boy's wages..............................	180	0	0
To Maistry's wages..............................	336	0	0
To fern and other weeds for making manure..	200	0	0
Rs.	4,716	0	0

4th Year.

Same as third year.......................Rs.	4,716	0	0
Return of 3rd year, 1,000 maunds at 7 Rs. per maund.......................... „	7,000	0	0
Return of 4th year, 4,000 maunds at 7 Rs. per maund.......................... „	28,000	0	0
Rs.	35,000	0	0
Expended 1st 4 years....	20,939	0	0
Profit......Rs.	14,061	0	0

In this estimate, the wages, &c. have been estimated at the current rate. The coolie lines and cattle shed are of the commonest and cheapest kind, consequently they will have to be renewed every 3rd year ; it would be a great saving of labour, though of course more expensive at the outset, if the buildings were pucka built and roofed with corrugated zinc.

Here is what might be done in most of the planting localities in Southern India, by an enterprising individual with a moderate capital to start with.

	Rs	A.	P.
1 Cost of land (100 acres)...................	1,000	0	0
2 Cost of planting 20,000 trees...............	500	0	0
3 Planter's living for the first year, and the getting up of a nursery, &c.............	2,000	0	0
4 Planter's living for 2nd year,..............	2,000	0	0
5 Building a dwelling house, to be completed by the second year....................	2,000	0	0
6 Purchase of cattle.........................	1,000	0	0
7 Pigs, Poultry, &c.........................	500	0	0
8 Building of a puckah cow-shed............	500	0	0
9 Building proper farm yard................	500	0	0
Total Rs..	10,000	0	0

Thus, at the end of the 2nd year of sojourn on the intended plantation, the planter will find himself with a good house to live in, and in the possession of 50 head of cattle, a well stocked farm-yard, a well filled manure pit, and 20,000 trees planted out thriving.

THIRD YEAR'S EXPENDITURE.

	Rs.	A.	P.
To up-keep of plantation..................	600	0	0
For planter's living.......................	1,200	0	0
	1,800	0	0
For 4th and 5th year's expenses, say........	3,600	0	0
	5,400	0	0
Bring forward amount of expenditure for the 1st and 2nd years....................	10,000	0	0
Total Rs...	15,400	0	0

At the end of 5 years, the plantation will yield on an average 1,000 maunds of marketable coffee, which at 6 Rs. the maund will yield 6,000 Rs., deducting 1,000 Rs. for up-keep and other contingencies. The planter's income would be 5,000 Rs. per annum.

In explanation it may be necessary to state, that I have put down for the planter's living 100 Rs. and 50 Rs. monthly for house-rent; with this amount, judging from living in most of the planting localities, any planter—nay, a married couple with a small family, might live very comfortably, more especially when we take into account the products obtainable from the farm yard.

In the purchase of cattle I should secure none but good milch cows and buffaloes. A very good milch cow or buffaloe with a young calf at her side may be purchased for 35 Rs. The planter should purchase his cattle gradually as opportunities offer. The better plan would be to buy a few in milk, and about the time they run dry to secure others.

By a pucka built cow house, I mean one built with stone walls, chunamed and enclosed with a substantially built wall; and roofed with corrugated zinc. The poultry yard, pig stye, &c, should be of the same kind. The cost of land varies in different localities, and of late has been rising in value greatly. I have put down the value at 10 Rs. the acre.

This estimate is not made from mere theory, but has resulted from practical experience, in one or two instances, and I have no hesitation in commending it to intending planters.

CHAPTER VII.

Diseases to which the Coffee plant is subject, and Animals destructive to it.—To make this subject clear, it will first be necessary to know what constitutes a healthy condition of the coffee plant, in order to discover the presence of disease.

The coffee plant when regularly grown and pruned forms a very handsome bush, and in a state of health is well covered with dark green foliage. The leaves are from 3 to 5 inches long and nearly 2 broad, having a wavy margin and beautiful glossy appearance, and as already described, when in bloom the flowers form white clusters at the base of the leaves or nodes, and possess a pleasing odour. Every part of the plant should be well formed, and indicate the presence of health and vigour as it passes through its different stages of growth ; it should yield its maiden crop in the third year of its existence, in favored localities, and should increase in productiveness and vigour with age.

It is necessary to remember that there are two states in the life of a plant inimical to health. The first consists in an excess of moisture in the soil, which not only renders the plant dropsical and favours the formation of soft sappy wood with a superabundance of foliage—this excess of moisture diluting the sap—but diverts it towards the wood and leaves, rendering the plant sterile or very scantily fruitful, from a tendency to succulence. Should this occur when the plant is in flower, the fruit either becomes abortive or does not ripen, but dries in an immature state, and these imperfect and blackened berries will be found adherent to the bushes for a long time ere they are cast off, and in the few berries that form, on examination the bean is found rotten and black ; this state arises from the sap bearing vessels being gorged with the diluted secretion, when they become ruptured and the nutrition to the plant is cut off.

Instances of the immature fruits drying on the bushes, or of the bean rotting in the cherry, are not wanting in those localities where there is an excess of moisture ; planters are familiar with this state of things, but are evidently ignorant of the cause or remedy. The remedy consists in thoroughly cleansing the soil of weeds, and opening out the soil in the vicinity of the plants ; if it could be carried out through the plantation so much the better, and where the moisture is still persistent, by draining the plantation. By opening out the soil we favour evaporation of the moisture, and when plants from this cause become sterile, their main roots should be opened out and exposed to the sun, in a similar manner to that practised on grape vines, which will tend to concentrate the sap and render the plant prolific.

This should be done a month or two prior to the flowering season, and should the season at the time prove dry, 24, 36, or 48 hours exposure will suffice, but sometimes 3 or 4 days may be necessary ; after the exposure, the roots should be covered in by fine soil and manure.

Secondly.—The same results may arise from an opposite cause ; namely, the want of a due proportion of moisture in the sap to maintain the integrity of the plant, and thus a shrinking of the sap vessels occurs—owing to which the plants become stunted in growth, their leaves hang loosely, and their dark green glossy color changes to a pale yellow colour ; for the sap taken up by the roots reaches the leaves, and is thus exposed to air and light, and a large transpiration of the watery fluid takes place. It does not seem to be generally understood that the more elevated a place the plant occupies, its action in proportion decreases, because the air is less dense, and from being colder has a greater evaporative power. Notwithstanding this, no care is evinced to shade and protect the plants, in the more exposed localities in which they are grown. The direct effect of the sun's rays even in these hilly regions has already been alluded to, so that the absorption of water by the roots is unable to keep pace with the evaporation going on. The Arab, from experience, seems to understand this better, and protects his plantation on exposed situations, by planting sparely over the plantation, fruit, timber, or other useful trees, which not only shade the coffee plants from the direct effects of the sun, but attract and preserve moisture. The planter in India, on the contrary, seems to denude not only the plantation but its vicinity of trees ; even those that overhang and protect the hill streams are cut down, and the result is soon seen in the drying up of these streams, which it should have been the planter's interest carefully to cherish and protect.

In one or two places I had opportunities of pointing out to several gentlemen the pernicious system that I found practised, by demonstrating the fact of several streams then lying dry, through the destruction of trees in their vicinity.

Any one anxious to convince himself by ocular demonstration, has only to visit the Shevaroy hills and examine the several plantations there, and he will find that whilst all those plantations protected by neighbouring hills or trees are in a high state of health, with that beautiful glossy dark green color so peculiar to the coffee plant, those in elevated and exposed places are looking yellow and sickly, frequently with dwarfed leaves.

It will thus be seen that cultivated plants are subject to an invariable tendency to disease, from 2 opposite causes. The excessive developement of any particular structure is liable to destroy the equilibrim of the whole plant with reference to its secretions, and this may result from physical causes existing either in the soil or climate of the locality in which it is grown. On the other hand it may arise from starvation, or from a state of semi-starvation; the plant being wholly or partially deprived of the necessary ingredients for its nourishment.

In the one case starving the plant into dwarfishness, in the other developing it into sappy luxuriance.

These states require only to be understood and they can readily be corrected, by modifying the effects of the climate to a certain extent, and gradually acclimatizing the plant to its situation, or by supplying the soil with the necessary ingredients of water, manure, &c.

The coffee plants cannot stand cold, more particularly during frosty weather. Plants that were healthy and thriving, will sometimes be found blasted and withered in one night, more particularly in the vicinity of streams or reservoirs of water, consequently coffee does not as a rule thrive beyond an altitude of 5,000 feet.

In the suggestion of shading plantations on exposed situations, sufficient attention has not been paid to shelter, for we often see the whole face of a mountain planted seemingly without any regard to this, and whenever the monsoon bursts upon the land, or even when strong winds sweep through the gorges of the hills, the plants become stunted in growth, the trees bare of branches, and the produce is small; to remedy which, planting of trees was recommended, in doing which much care and forethought is necessary, for if the plantation be crowded with trees, the coffee plants will grow lanky, and probably will not fruit well. I find from Labourier's "Treatise on coffee planting in the W. Indies," that coffee has been successfully cultivated with the plantain, which is not by any means a bad spec, except that they are rather fragile in structure, and from the height they attain, of 12 and 15 feet, they are likely to be thrown down, with loss to themselves and injury to the coffee plant; but there is a variety called the "Mauritius plantain,"* procurable at Ponidcherry, I believe, which never attains more than four feet in height, the stem is robust, and the fruit tasty and well flavored, and even when ripe the skin preserves its green color, and does not change into yellow. They form large bunches, each comb of which is well covered—the fruit is stout and well formed. The introduction of this variety of the plantain, and interspersing it over those plantations that are greatly exposed, would prove decidedly advantageous to the coffee, and the return made by the plantain itself would add to the planter's profits. Other fruit trees, such as the orange, loquot, pear, apple, &c., might with advantage be planted over the plantation in like manner. The palma christi or castor oil plant† in particular might be planted, and would be suitable in every respect, as well as profitable. We should bear in mind that coffee will only thrive luxuriantly under the protection and shade of some trees, whilst others are likely to prove injurious to it, from the excretions they throw out, from time to time, which if they do not kill the plant at once, may render it sickly, although food suitable to its nourishment abounds; this can only be ascertained by the result of experience and observation. Where possible, belts of forest should be allowed to exist upon the ridges to shelter the plantations.

Plants, like animals, are subject to ravages from parasites. Of those I have met with, are the various lichens, mosses and some kinds of ferns, which cover the stem of the plant from

---

* Musă Cavendishïi.

† Recinus communis—on the Shervaroys I met some of these growing into huge trees, attaining 20 and 30 feet in height, and the stem 8 to 12 inches in diameter.

top to bottom, much to its injury. Even in those instances where they do not interfere with the nourishment of the plant, they crowd the stem and deprive it of that free circulation of air which is so necessary for its healthy existence, and also take up the moisture and other fertilizing influences of the atmosphere, whilst some few live entirely at the expense of the plant, and if once allowed to take possession of it, they will in a short time spread over every part and greatly interfere with its health and luxuriance. The only effectual way of destroying these parasites, is by occasionally sending coolies into the plantation to examine the trees, and free them of all such parasites, and if the necessary attention be given to the plant with reference to a free circulation of air by the removal of weeds, and attention to pruning, that excess of moisture will be prevented from forming to the injury and consequent sterility of the tree, and to the favouring of parasitic growth, for free exposure to light and air is the greatest enemy to parasites, be they animal or vegetable.

Animals and insects injurious to the coffee plant.

As far as my own experience extends, what is popularly known by planters as the "coffee-bug" is the greatest enemy to the coffee plant, and these will be found to infest those plantations where moisture abounds, whether arising from the surface or soil.

Through the kindness of a friend, I have been favoured with specimens of these from different places, such as Coorg, Wynaad, &c. and I find that all the specimens are the same. A species of "*coccus*" which I have taken the liberty to name the "*coccus coffeæ*," but in Sir J. E. Tennant's Ceylon, vol. ii. page 268, he says that Walker has named it the "Lecanium Coffeæ." "It establishes itself on the young shoots and buds, which it covers with a noisome incrustation of scales enclosing its larva, from the pernicious influence of which the fruit shrivels and drops off. It is a coccus, and a number of brownish wart-like bodies may be seen studding the young shoots and buds, and occasionally the margins on the under side of the leaves. Each of these warts is a transformed female containing a large number of eggs (700), which are batched within it. When the young ones come out of their nest, they may be observed running about on the plant, looking like wood lice. Shortly after being hatched, the males seek the under side of the leaves, while the females prefer the young shoots as their place of abode. The larva of the males undergoes transformation into pupæ beneath their own skins, their wings are horizontal, the possessing wings may probably explain the comparatively rare presence of the male on the bushes." "The female retains her powers of locomotion until nearly her full size, and it is about this time that her impregnation takes place. "The pest does not produce great injury until it has been two or three years on an estate; but at length the scales on the plants become numerous, the clusters of berries assume a black sooty look, and a great number of them fall off before they are mature; the young shoots have a disgusting look from the number of yellow pustular bodies forming on them; the leaves get shrivelled, and on many trees not a single berry forms. The Coffee bug first appeared in 1843 on the *Lupallu Galla* estate, and it or a closely allied species has been observed on the Citrus acida, Psidium pomiferum, Myrtus Zeylanica, Rosa indica, Careya arborea, Vitex Negundoo, and other plants, and most abundantly on the coffee bushes in moist places. It re-appears though eradicated. Dr. Gardner, whom Sir J. E. Tennant quotes, is of opinion that all remedies have failed, and that it must wear itself out as other blights do." Such is the account as quoted by Balfour's Cyclopædia, Supplement, Vol. II.

The "Coccus Coffeæ," and according to Walker the "Lecanium Coffeæ*" belongs to Class VIII, Insecta, Order IV, Rhynchota.

The Coccus Coffeæ was examined by me, from specimens received from a friend, which he procured from some of the estates at Wynaad and "Coorg." The stem back of the leaves and the young shoots are covered with small oval or rounded bodies, having the appearance of a shield, owing to which no part of the insect, but these little warty projections only are visible, being about the size of a grain of barley and globular as a pea, and firmly adherent to the stem, of which if they once take possession it seems difficult to exterminate them, The effect of these visitants on the plant is curious. The tree seems paralysed, growth is stopped, the leaves turn black, and are covered with a fine black dust. The blossom shews as usual, but scarcely so abundant as in a healthy plant, and when the berries are formed they will not ripen, but dry on the tree, and the bean in the few cherries that do form is rotten. Some plants are rendered perfectly sterile. In those I examined, the wart-like protuberance had become apparently converted into a shell, and on being touched by the finger broke, and displayed a white downy substance filled with ova and young, some of the latter under the microscope were found to possess six short feet, and were seen to move pretty actively ; the eyes were small, dark, and prominent, and the insect itself of a mealy brown colour, and it is like that I have found to exist on the cotton plant—it contained the minute seta or rostrum for puncturing the plant. The only differences I found to exist between the bug found on the coffee and that found on the cotton plant were, that in the coffee the outer covering was oval, consistent and shell-like, and the colour mealy brown, while in the cotton the covering was

---

* From *LeKane*, a bason ; alluding to the form of the shields or incrustations.

soft and downy and somewhat irregular, and streaked with greyish white. This is a great pest to the coffee plant, and is familiar to the planter under the name of the "*coffee bug*," and is found extremely injurious to the coffee plant, whilst they are remarkable for their powers of propogation. In those that I examined, each wart-like excrescence was swarming with ova and young —No remedy has been tried, and the planters aware that any remedy however simple must involve an immense outlay, consider it best to let it run its course, and in time the plant recovers of itself, but not before two or more crops are sacrificed. Norton's deodorizing fluid will be found the best remedy for the coffee-bug ; my experimentson the cotton and other plants lead me to this conclusion ; and it is well worthy of a trial. The fluid should be sprinkled over the plant freely, and the parts infested with the bug be brushed over with a solution. It in no way injures the tree ; on the contrary is an acquisition to the soil or manure, and the fluid is sufficiently cheap to allow of its receiving a fair trial.

ORDER XI.

Hymenoptera.

Suborder I. Sciurifera.—The Phyllophaga or saw fly, popularly known to the planter as the "coffee fly." These insects are extremely destructive and the mischief frequently is not known till the plant is seen to wither and die, more particularly the tender shoots which are punctured and the ova deposited in them and the young larva burrows in these, feeding on the pith and other tissues. By the time it has attained maturity, several inches of the branch will have been eaten through, and the nutrition of the plant arrested, so that it soon begins to wither away. If now examined, the empty shell or bark of the branch will only be found to exist.

The xylophaga or tailed wasp belonging to the second

tribe of this order, proves extremely mischievous by burrowing in the wood of the stem and branches of the coffee plant, and causing its destruction.

There are I believe several other larva of Dipeterous and Lepidopterous insects that prove injurious to the coffee plant, but my experience is limited, so that I cannot say much on this subject.

Class IV. Aves.

Order V. Columbæ.

Of this order the Green,* beetle wing,† Imperial,‡ and other pigeons feed in some localities on the coffee berries. It is I believe only the absence of other fruits in the vicinity that makes them take to the coffee berries occasionally, but one can imagine what depredations would be committed by a large body of pigeons alighting on a plantation daily.

Order IV.

Pachydermata.

Of this order the wild hog or *Sus Scrofa* is extremely destructive to the coffee plantation, for it not only roots up the soil to the injury of the coffee bushes, but devours the fruits also, as I have myself witnessed. In their attempts to get at the ripe berries they will often bite off branches and twigs; they sometimes injure the plants by brushing against them, thus not only injuring the bark, but throwing down flowers and young fruits.

Order VI.

Ruminantia.

Sheep, deer, buffaloes, and cows will not touch the coffee plant, but goats occasionally do.

History attributes the discovery of the qualities of coffee

* Columbæ Elphinstonii.

† Vinago bicincta.

‡ Alsocornus puniceus.

to the browsing of goats on the coffee berries* and it is possible that they may relish the ripe berries better than the leaves, owing to the saccharine flavour and taste in the fruits, but most of the other animals, although they do not feed on the plant, should not be allowed to enter a plantation, as they go about brushing against the plants, they injure and bruise the tender leaves, and throw down the flowers or fruit. And cattle, especially buffaloes, are in the habit of rubbing themselves against the stem, frequently peeling off the bark and breaking the branches and twigs, in addition to what has been detailed above.

ORDER VIII.

Rodents.

The muridæ or rat family are extremely destructive to the coffee berries; they are very fond of the pulp of the berries, which they greedily devour, and at the same time throw down the seeds. These depredations are generally committed at night, when they climb the plants and creep along the stem in search of the berry. This is more particularly applicable to the field or coffee rat, the *Mus Hirsutus* of W. Elliot† which infests plantations, burrowing in the soil, and frequently injuring the roots of the coffee plants in excavating its retreats in the ground.

SCIURIDÆ.

The *sciurus cinerus* or common grey squirrel of Southern India is destructive to coffee plantations, which they ravage in search of the ripe berries, and in some localities what are termed the Hill squirrels, the *Sciurus maximus*, creates some damage, but as far as I am aware, the damage done by

---

* Another version states that the discovery of coffee was owing to the reports of a Camel driver to the Prior of a Maronites convent that his Camels could get no sleep after having browsed on the coffee plant. Vide Dr. J. Scofferns outlines of Botany, p. 121.

† Golunda Ellioti of Gray.

squirrels and rats extends only to the pulpy part of the berries.

Order X.

Carnivora.

Of this order the common jackal or *canis aureus*, is destructive to the coffee berries, but the fruits are swallowed entire and the bean passes through them uninjured. The *Paradoxurus typhus*, more familiarly known by the Tamil name of *Maranáy*, literally wood dog, by some as toddy cat, is a great pest to the coffee plantation, particularly when it is in fruit, as it lives for the most part on these occasions on coffee berries, lodging in holes or trees or in the crevices of rocks in the day, and turning out at night in search of food ; it lives on both vegetable and animal food. It is particularly destructive to fruits of every description. It belongs to the order Feræ, family Felidæ, and sub-family viverrinæ.

Order XI.

Chiroptera.

Of this order the Flying fox or *Pteropus edulis* is the chief,* but these are not met with in all places ; they are extremely destructive to fruits in general, and only occasionally take the coffee berries.

Order XV.

Quadrumana.

Of this order all families of Monkeys are destructive to coffee plantations. Of these the, *Presbytes, Eentellus*, or Hanuman, the *Silenus veter* or wanderoo, the, *Macacus Cynomolgus* and *M. Radiatus*, are the chief, these animals are great pests to all plantations, for they not only devour the tender leaves, but wantonly throw down quantities of

---

* There is a smaller kind of bat the Pteropus hese hen aulti which also feeds freely on the coffee berry.

berries, break the twigs, and throw down the leaves, and in their jumping from bush to bush break branches, and throw down flowers and immature fruits, and thus commit an incredible amount of damage on coffee estates, if allowed to enter plantations.

CHAPTER VIII.

The Medicinal, Chemical, and Physiological properties of Coffee.—The medicinal properties of coffee in the form prepared for ordinary use, have not been fully taken advantage of, but it is to be hoped that it will be more largely used as a remedy in diseases.

" Coffee both in its raw and roasted states has been the subject of repeated chemical investigations."

" Raw coffee must he slightly nutritious, on account of the gum and other nutritive principles which it contains. Rasori employed it like powdered bark, in intermittent fever, and Grindel used it in other cases ,also as a substitute for cinchona. By roasting, its nutritive principles are for the most part destroyed, while the empyreumatic matters developed communicate a stimulant influence with respect to the nervous system."

" Roasted coffee possesses powerful anti-soporific properties ; hence its use as a drink by those who desire nocturnal study, and as an antidote to counteract the effects of opium and other narcotics, and to relieve intoxication. In those unaccustomed to its use, it is apt to occasion thirst and constipation."

" I know a lady on whom it acts as a purgative."

" It is sometimes very useful in relieving head-ache. It has also been employed as a febrifuge in intermittents, as a stomachic in some forms of dyspepsia, as an astringent in Diarrhœa, and as a stimulant to the cerebro spinal system, in some nervous disorders. Floyer, Dr. Percival, and others, have used it in spasmodic asthma, and Læunic (Treat. on diseases of the chest by Forbes, 2nd Ed. p. 418) says I have myself seen several cases in which coffee was really useful."*

Dr. W. Hamilton recommends the free use of strong coffee as almost a specific for calculous complaints, more especially when connected with gout and rheumatism, and Dr. Mosely has observed in his Treatise on coffee, that—

" The great use of coffee in France is supposed to have abated the prevalence of gravel. In French colonies where coffee is more used than in the English, as well as in Turkey where it is the principal beverage, not only gravel, but the gout, those tormentors of the human race, are scarcely known. Du-Four relates as an extraordinary instance of the effects of coffee in gout, the case of M. Deverau. He says this gentleman was attacked with gout at twenty-five years of age, and had it severely till he was upwards of fifty, with chalk stones in the joints of his hands and feet ; but for four years preceding the account of his case being given to Du-Four to lay before the public, he had been recommended the use of coffee, which he adopted, and had no return of the gout afterwards. But its efficacy is not confined to the cure of these maladies, Sir John Floyer, who had suffered under asthma for more than sixty years, without finding relief from any of the numerous remedies he tried, was at length cured, when above eighty years of age, by the free use of coffee."†

‡ Royle says, " It is too well known for its stimulating or rousing influence on the brain, especially to those unaccustomed to its use."

" Hence it is employed as a cerebral stimulant, and antisoporific, and to counteract the effects of opium and other narcotic po isons."

* Pereira's Materia Medica, vol. vi. page 1031.

† Royle's Materia Medica, 3rd Ed. by Dr. Headland, page 478.

‡ Grey's Pharmacalogia 3rd Ed. page 90.

" The fresh seeds are, febrifuge, diuretic, and tonic ; when roasted they acquire a sweet scented empyreumatic oil,which is heating to the body, and a small portion of tanning matter. They are then well known to form a stomachic, anti-hypnotic infusion, which stimulates the nervous system."*

Both strong coffee and green tea have been recommended in poisoning by opium or alcohol. We have known these agents to be employed with success under both circumstances.†

Dr. Leslie believes that coffee is beneficial in strangulated hernia. Vide vol. iii. page 198, Madras Quarterly Journal of Medical Science.

My own experience enables me to say, that I have frequently had opportunities of using a strong infusion of coffee in cases of poisoning by opium and stramonium, with decided benefit, and in asthma in many instances have I witnessed its beneficial effects. As an external application in foul and offensive sores, I have found considerable benefit from its use as a lotion ; it at once corrects the foul smell that arises from cancerous and other malignant ulcers, and acts as a mild stimulant to the part.

" The berry (vulgoc offee) when dried and burnt, is tonic and stimulant. In small doses a strong decoction of coffee is capable of arresting diarrhœa, whilst in large doses it acts as a cathartic. Dr. Pickford attributes this partly to the action of the motar nerves, which being weakened, are by its moderate stimulus restored to their normal condition; and thereby Diarrhœa depending on their deranged condition is relieved. When large doses are taken, the motar nerves become over stimulated ; and on this increased action arises an increased amount of alvine secretion. He considers also that coffee undoubtedly possesses the property of pro-

---

* **Pharmaceutical Journal, vol. xiii. page, 330.**

† Vide Lancet, No. xviii vol. i 2d May 1863 page 512.

moting digestion and of increasing the biliary secretion. This last opinion is in accordance with Liebeg's views, who points out the singular fact that caffeine, the peculiar principle of coffee, is identical with Theine the peculiar principle of tea ; and that both these substances, with the addition of oxygen and the elements of water, can yield Saurine' the nitrogenized compound peculiar to bile. It is of importance as a means of disguising the tastes of nauseous medicines, particularly quinine, senna, and epsom salts."

" *Therapeutic uses.* Coffee is highly recommended in *spasmodic asthma*, as an infusion, in *Infantile cholera, Bilious diarrhœa*, in the *vomiting of pregnancy*, in *Tic Douloureux, Hemicrania*, and *other neuralgic Head affections, Intermittent and other fevers, Hay Fever* or *Hay asthma, Hooping cough, poisoning* by *opium, Aconite*, and *other narcotic Poisons.* A strong infusion of coffee without milk or sugar is an effectual stimulant, and is advantageously given in the *depression* after *drunkenness*, and in *nervous* and *hysterical head-aches.* Vide Warning's Therapeutics, 1854, pages 162, 3 and 4."

The disinfectant properties of coffee have long been known. It is useful to purify any place having an offensive smell or foul air. The coffee beans should be roasted in the vicinity of the room to be purified, and when they have attained their brown color and while quite hot, removed to the room and placed in the centre, in the same pan or chattie in which they were torrified ; the doors and windows should be closed, and in half an hour, by which time the coffee will have become cool, the room will be found thoroughly purified and the air rendered sweet.

This property of purifying foul air is evidently dependant on the essential oil given out during the torrifaction of the bean. I have frequently had recourse to coffee as a disinfectant, with success

Physiological effects of Coffee.—The effects of coffee on the system are mainly dependant on three of its chief constituents ; viz., 1st.—the volatile oil formed during the torrifaction of the bean, 2nd.—The tannic acid. And 3rd,—The caffeine ; whilst the other constituents of coffee are gum, resin, fixed oil, extractive albumen, and lignin. We shall here briefly consider the three essential ingredients on which the plysiological action of this now world renowned bean depends.

Volatile Oil.—The volatile oil is procured by the distillation of roasted coffee, which, when taken internally, has been found to produce a pleasing excitement and a sensible perspiration. It is also very refreshing after fatigue, and when taken in large quantities it produces wakefulness, more especially in those unaccustomed to its use. Sometimes it is believed to act as a sedative on the heart and bloo d vessels. Dr. Billing explains the sedative effects in relieving stupor produced by stimulants, or the drowsiness of fatigue or other plethora, by counteracting this action on the brain, and restoring it to a normal state by continued stimulation.* This volatile oil seems formed during the torrifaction of the coffee bean, and although it is present in a small quantity, which is believed to be one pound to one hundred thousand, and the oil is produced during torrifaction, it is not exactly known what principle of the raw coffee produces it.†

Secondly.—We come to tannin or tannic acid : this is, when pure, white, but generally has a yellowish tinge, and differs from other acids of a similar kind, in rendering a solution of iron green instead of black. The tannin is formed during the roasting of coffee by the action of heat.‡

---

* Royle's Materia Medica, page 327.

† Blackwood's Magazine, No. ccoclix, vol. lxxv, January 1854, page 105.

‡ Ibid.

Thirdly.—We come to caffeine, which is a crystallizable substance devoid of alkaline properties, and is found in the coffee according to the different varieties, yielding from two to four pounds in every hundred.* Its composition is C 4, H 2½, N.O.†

The quantities of caffeine in 100 parts of different varieties of coffee, are as follows :—

		Caffeine.
Martinique	coffee	6·4
Alexandria	ditto	4·4
Java	ditto	4·4
Mocha	ditto	4·0
Cayenne	ditto	3·8
St. Domingo	ditto	3·2‡

" Chemical changes of coffee. Raw coffee according to Schrader consists of—

Peculiar coffee principle	17· 58
Gummy and mucilaginous extract	3· 64
Extractive	0· 62
Resin	0· 41
Fatty oil	0· 52
Solid residue	66· 66
Loss (water?)	10· 57
	100· 00

but on being roasted, coffee loses about one-fifth of its weight, but increases to nearly half its size. It is during the roasting process that the aroma is developed, varying with the manner and time in which the bean is roasted."

---

* Blackwood's Magazine, No. ccccliх, vol. lxxv, January 1854, page 105.

† Pereira's Materia Medica 1840 vol. ii, page 1031.

‡ Thompson's Organic Chemistry 1838, page 769.

Roasted coffee consists of—

Coffee principle	12· 50
Extractive	4· 80
Gum and mucilage	10· 42
Oil and resin	2· 08
Solid residue	68· 75
Loss	1· 45
	100· 00

Pfaff asserted that the aroma given out by roasted coffee depends on volatilization or decomposition of a peculiar acid, contained in raw coffee, and which has been denominated caffeic acid.*

The roasting of coffee.—As much as the aroma is said to depend on the peculiarity of soil and climate, much more depends on the manner of roasting or torrifying the coffee bean ; for simple as this operation may seem, it requires great nicety and judgement to torrify it to the required point and no further. The raw coffee, as must be known to all, is entirely free of aroma of any kind, but on being placed on a frying pan placed over the fire, the watery constituents of the bean are driven off as steam, whilst the coffee soon after gives out a fragrant odour, and the color changes to a light brown, and by the time the water has been driven off it becomes brown, with a peculiar burnt or coffee smell, and the beans will now be found to have increased somewhat in bulk, and some of them to have burst or cracked.

According to Professor Donovan as quoted by Porter,† there are 5 distinct stages, "1st the evaporation of the water, 2nd the formation of the colourless acid water, 3rd the production of yellow acid water, 4th the appearance of

* Pereira's Materia Medica, 1840 vol. ii, page 1031.

† Vide the Tropical Agriculturist, by G. R. Porter, page 77.

oil; and 5th the conversion of the coffee into charcoal, and destruction of its bitter principle."

The first three stages are not to be depended on, as it will require something beyond ordinary knowledge and scientific apparatus to carry out. All that is required is a little practical experience, so as not to carbonize the bean, but take it off the fire as soon as it attains a sufficiently deep brown colour. Various apparatus have been invented for roasting coffee, but I have never seen anything better than a frying pan or open chatty. Small quantities of the bean should be put in at one time and be constantly stirred, to prevent any one portion being more burned than another.

The heat should be moderate and uniform throughout the torrifaction, and care should be taken that no green or smoking wood be used, but wood that is well dried and will give a clear bright heat without smoke; otherwise the coffee is likely to take on a smoky or empyreumatic odour, which will spoil the flavour of the drink.

Preparation of the Bean.—The bean should be torrified in small quantities as required, but a week's supply may be prepared at a time. As soon as the bean has been torrified it should be finely powdered, and be preserved in a canister or stopper bottle, and a small weight of lead fitting to the circumference of the phial or to the square of the canister should be placed on the powder, so as to press it down, which will preserve its moisture and prevent fermentation. Most of the coffee mills in use merely bruise the coffee into a coarse grit, whereas by finely powdering coffee, every part readily comes in contact with the fluid when infused, and the infusion can be drawn off much sooner than when coarse grits are made use of.

Professor Donovan thus describes the preparation of coffee. "The whole water to be used is to be divided into two equal parts, one of which is to be drawn on the coffee but in an inverted order. In the usual order, boiling water is allowed to cool on coffee but if this be inverted, cold water should be heated on coffee over the fire until it come to a boil, and then it is to be removed. There is no difference between this and the usual method of infusion, as regards the retaining of the aroma, but it differs much with regard to the advantage of obtaining the liquid coffee at the end of the process, boiling hot instead of cold, and thus making a reheating necessary, which is always injurious. As soon as the liquor comes to a boil, it should be allowed to subside a few seconds, and must then be poured off as clear as it will run. The remaining half of the water at a boiling heat is immediately to be poured on the grounds; the vessel is to be placed on the fire, and kept boiling for about three minutes. This will extract all the bitterness left in the grounds, and after a few moments subsidence the clear part is to be poured off and mixed with the former liquor.—This mixed liquor now contains in perfection all the qualities which originally existed in the roasted coffee, and it is as hot as any taste can desire it. The boiling here recommended with the second half of the water, cannot be detrimental to the aromatic and volatile portions of the coffee, which have been already removed and secured in the infused portion."

The French are considered not only the largest consumers of coffee, but also great experts in the preparation of the beverage. The great secret of success is, that the coffee bean should be the best procurable. All damaged seeds should be removed, and the bean itself roasted in small quantities in an open frying pan, whilst it should constantly, from the time the beans are placed on the fire until when they are taken out, be stirred about so as to give the seed a light brown colour, by which time it will have lost about one-sixth in weight, when it should be powdered in a mortar or mill. Sufficient for one day only should be prepared at a time, as by keeping, coffee loses more or less of its flavour. To two ounces of powder add a pint of boiling water, and set it aside until it settles—then strain.

I have been in the habit of using a cold infusion of coffee, which is thus prepared. Over night place 2 ounces of coffee powder in a saucepan or jug, and pour over it a pint of cold water and set it aside; in the morning the infusion is strained off, heated, and boiling milk added, or what is better, warmed first and then strained.

The "*café au lait*" that I have tasted in Paris, and been at some pains to become initiated in the manufacture of, is thus prepared. To from 3 to 4 oz. of coffee powder, add a pint of boiling water; let it stand for about 10 minutes, and strain; fill about one-third of the cup with the infusion, and fill the cup with fresh boiling milk; sweeten to taste.

Various ingredients are used to clear the coffee, among which may be named, isinglass, fish skin, white of egg, or by pouring a half cup of cold water into the boiling liquid, and an endless variety of coffee pots have been invented for making coffee, but as far as my own personal experience extends, I have found nothing to equal a covered jug and a piece of flannel made into a bag, and fitted into a wire or bamboo ring. The coffee is placed in the jug and the necessary quantity of water poured on it, and covered for about 10 minutes; then strain through the flannel bag; the coffee thus prepared will be as clear and as good as that from any patent coffee pot, provided the necessary attention has been given to roasting, powdering, and quantity of coffee used; and especial care should be taken to see that the water is *boiling*.

The flannel strainer should be turned inside out and well washed and dried in the sun after use, daily, and will then last many months.

CHAPTER IX.

The Collection of the Produce and the preparation of it for the Market.—The crop begins to ripen from November to January and as soon as the plants give indications of having ripened their fruits, preparations should be made for picking the crop, and where labour is plentiful and readily procurable, it would be a good plan to send in men, women, and children above 10 years of age, to collect the ripe fruit; and none but those that are ripe and have passed through the various shades of color and become purple, should be taken off daily; this would in a measure lighten the bushes and enable the remaining tender and young fruits to advance to maturity more readily, and if picked out as they ripen, a quantity will be saved from birds and animals. But the planter cannot always adopt this system, as he may not at all times be able to procure labour, and consequently he waits until the greater part of the bushes have ripened, before employing people to collect the crop.

Various systems have been employed; some contracting for the work at so much an acre—others contract for so much the bushel or Ton, &c., others employ coolies, giving them their daily hire; each of these systems has its advantages and disadvantages. Coolies will be anxious to hurry over work performed on contract, with the hope of gaining time to take another job, and thus they will not only injure the plants, but throw down much of the tender and unripe fruits, and if it be made daily work, they will prolong it as much as possible; but by effective, supervision these may be remedied. Of these different systems, daily task work is much the best, for then each cooly, although paid by the day, will have to produce so much coffee at the end of his work, and will thus be made to exhibit a fair day's labour. One man, when the plantation is well filled with fruit, can pick two bushels a day, and a woman from 1½ to 1¾ bushels, or from 25 to 30 measures, and a boy or girl from 1 to 1½ in a working day of from 8 to 9 hours; when task work is decided on, they should not be hurried, but be allowed slowly and within the given day's work to complete the quantity, and in the proportion to which they fall short, a small fine should be levied

Labour has risen considerably in the market, in consequence of the great demands made by various departments. The rate of wages a couple of years ago, was one rupee a week for a man, and 8 annas for women and boys. In some places it has now risen to 4 annas per day for a man, and one rupee a week for women, and on some occasions estates have paid as much as 5 and 6 annas per day, but these are rare instances. Great care is necessary to see that none but the thoroughly ripe berries are collected, and in the doing of which the unripe and tender fruits should in no way be injured. All cases in which injury has been done to the unripe fruits from carelessness, or when the unripe and tender fruits are picked off the bushes, should be severely punished by depriving the party of his day's wages; one or two examples will have the good effect of deterring others from doing the same. This, however, is not always successful, for when labour is in great demand, the threat of stopping their wages will at once induce them to strike work. It requires some tact and good management to deal with ignorant coolies.

Each coffee picker should be supplied with a small basket, or what is better a bag made of common dungary cloth, or where facilities exist they may be made of leather. If bags are supplied, they should be slung round the necks of the coolies, and as each picker fills his basket or bag, it should be emptied into a large basket placed in a central situation at an easy distance, to be handy to the gang.

Two or more baskets should be placed here, so that as they fill, they can be taken away to the pulping or drying house. If the latter, they should be spread on mats to dry, for if they are simply heaped together, they are likely to become sour or to ferment, and thus impart an unpleasant flavor to the bean. But the chief object in view is, by drying or pulping, to facilitate the separation of the bean from the pulp and testa. It has already been noticed that birds and animals are the greatest enemies that the coffee planter has to contend with in the realization of his crops, and it should be borne in mind that although this fruit is eaten, the seed or bean passes through entire and uninjured, consequently it would prove advantageous, and a large portion of the bean so lost would be recovered, if the plan detailed below were followed, and it would also tend to give fresh vigour to the plants, which will repay the planter for the additional labour, or it might be done at once in conjunction with weeding and pruning.

Immediately the crop is gathered in, and before the coolies have dispersed, they should be sent in with a supply of common coir cord, with which they gather together and gently tie the outspreading branches of the plants, while women and children are engaged to pick up the droppings of birds and animals, as well as any fruits that may have dropped from the plants themselves. Having tied up a portion of the plantation, the men return to the part they started from at first, and loosen carefully the soil around the plant, whilst the women and children convey manure to them, which in regulated quantities is placed in the excavation made round the tree, and covered in with soil, while the women go round undoing the trees that have been completed; when pruning may be performed, so that the whole of the process is carried out about the same time. The loosening of the soil gives vigour to the plants, and the monsoon when it sets in enables the earth to absorb a larger quantity of moisture than it would do otherwise, and the benefit to the plant is incalculable. Simply loosening the soil may be practised after the picking has been completed, leaving the manuring for a subsequent period, but it is far preferable to complete the operations for the season at once·

In some plantations, pucka built terraces are prepared for a drying ground ; in others, raised platforms covered over with common matting are got up temporarily for the purpose, and on these the berries are spread out, so as to profit both by sun and air. On other plantations the pulping mill of the kind about to be described is set up, for the purpose of freeing the pulp from the seed in its fresh state, and before it has time to get heated or fermented.

The pulping house is the building which covers the machine termed a pulper, and should be built in the vicinity of a stream, so as to have the command of water.

Pulping Machines.—Several of these have been invented from time to time, and improvements still continue to be carried out, but the machine known as "Gordon's Brest pulper" is now in general use, and seems to answer every purpose. It can be driven with the greatest facility, and requires no seive. It pulps the coffee much cleaner, and cuts or pricks less, than an ordinary sieve pulper. It pulps from 30 to 40 bushels per hour, and the advantage it possesses over most other machines is its extreme simplicity, for with a little care it seldom or ever gets out of order. It can be worked much faster than any other machine of its kind, and from the facility with which it can be drawn recommends itself. The coffee berry is only submitted once, and passes through clean. It is worked through a water box.

Another invention is thus given by Balfour, in his 2nd supplemental volume to the Cyclopædia of India, as taken from the "*Madras Times*" of 19th January 1859.

"Grey's Pea berry machine was satisfactorily introduced in 1858, at the St. Sebastian mills in Ceylon. It consists of three metal rollers, so placed beside each other, as to allow in their revolution the flat beans to pass between them, while the pea berries pass along the surface of the rollers into a box. This is regarded as a valuable addition to the means of those who prepare coffee for the European market, and who can by this machine meet the fancy for pea berry coffee, without the tedious employment of hand labour." The pulper is placed on two strong beams, and beneath it is the cistern, into which the coffee drops in its passage through the pulper. This operation of pulping continues worked by human or animal power, until the whole is completed. The coffee fruits are thrown into a hopper or wooden funnel located above the rollers, conducted by water, and dropping down between these, they are broken up by being stripped of their outer covering in pulp, and the double beans separated from each other; the bean on one side and the pulp on the other drop as they pass through, and the whole of the bean is now washed on to the adjacent cistern, by the turning on of the stream of water which fills the cistern, so as to allow of the coffee bean soaking for a night, and in the morning it is thoroughly washed to free it of the mucilaginous juice that covers it.

In building a pulping house, it is necessary therefore to lay your foundation for the cisterns, which should be built of wooden planks two inches thick, to prevent the wood from warping, and the joinings must be caulked to prevent leakage. Some planters prefer to have their cisterns built of brick and chunam, and occasionally we see cisterns with asphalte beds, which wear better than chunam beds. Experience, however, proves wood to be the best material for the construction of these cisterns.

The size of the cisterns must be in proportion to that of the plantation ; the general size suitable to most plantations being from 12 to 20 feet square each cistern, and about 3 feet in depth. The cisterns so constructed, should adjoin each other thus,

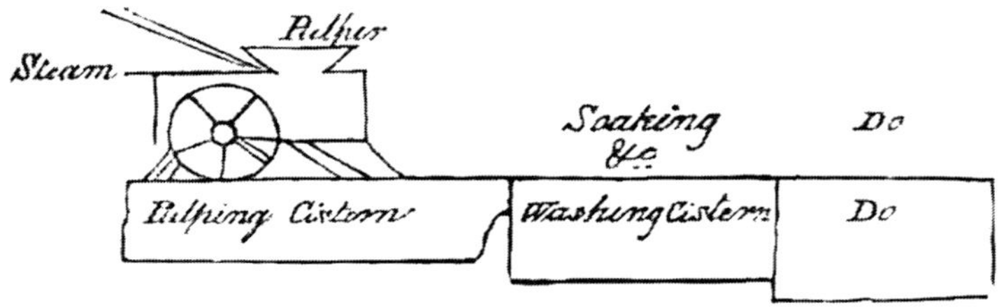

and little connecting doors a foot square, enable the coffee to be washed and passed into the adjoining cistern. Perforated zinc plates are placed against these openings, so as to facilitate the passage of the coffee or water from one cistern to another. They should be so constructed as to be in tiers one above the other, and allowing a difference of some 12 or 24 inches above the level of each other. The coffee when removed from the cisterns by coolies, some 12 or 18 hours after being pulped, is immediately put to dry in the sun in its parchment, and care is necessary to prevent any fermentation taking place. The drying ground is the next requisite, and should not be situated far from the cisterns, on the contrary should be as near as possible to them. This consists of a level or gentle slope, paved with brick and polished over with fine chunam. On this the coffee should be spread out to dry, and while drying, the bean should frequently be turned upside down.

This drying ground, although the cheapest and the one in general use, has one or two drawbacks. The large surface of coffee cannot be readily taken in, should a sudden shower of rain come down. Planters know how liable coffee districts are to such sudden down pours, and the coffee is likely to be affected by imbibing the earthy flavour from the chunam, unless the ground has been particularly well prepared. Drying on mats placed on platforms formed of stakes, some 3 or 4 feet above the ground, is sometimes had recourse to, and in a few instances the more expensive method of drying in zinc troughs running on castors, which can be rolled into the store room without trouble, but this of course could not be adopted where large crops of coffee have to be cured. Mr. W. H. Staines, of Coonoor, recommends the same on wheels ; one set above the other ; the trays running on rails, so that a touch sends them under cover.

The trays should be 15 + 15 or 20 + 12. Mr. Staines hopes to adopt this plan exclusively on his estates, in time.

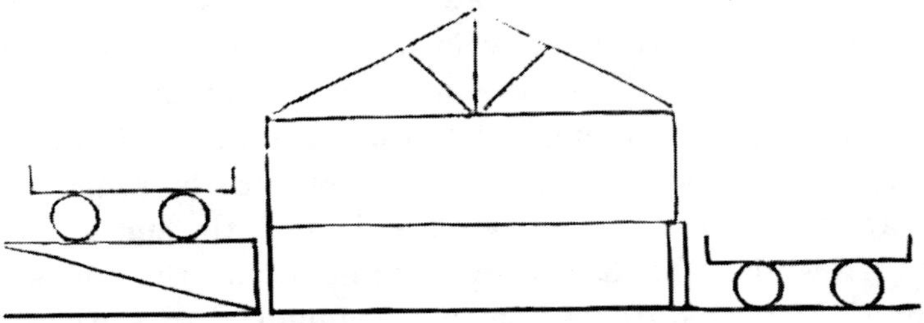

The next operation is that of milling the parchment coffee, to free the bean of its coriaceous membrane. This mill is sometimes termed the peeling mill, and consists of a wooden wheel which is turned vertically by animal power, by the yoking a pair of bullocks to its horizontal extremity. The wheel, which may be of wood or stone, is fitted to a circular groove, which is filled with the parchment coffee, and by the passage of the wheel over it, it bursts, and the parchment membrane which envelopes the bean is detached by its rapid rotatory movement.

In some rare instances other machines have been used for

this purpose, but not often. The bean is now winnowed to free it from its parchment, and to separate the bean from the chaff. On some estates the old wooden or stone mortars are still in use, for pounding the parchment coffee to free it from the chaff.

The Store House.—The coffee store house is a long building, suited to the size and wants of the estate, and is generally built of brick, and the floor boarded to keep out damp, these are usually called coffee godowns. The system of winnowing also differs. In some plantations the bean is taken up in basket fulls and thrown up against the wind. Whilst the coffee bean falls down by its weight, the membrane is carried away to some distance. Others employ women, who winnow away the chaff with the usual rice baskets or sieves, and some make use of a machine in which fans made of 4 or more pieces of tin or wooden planks, or tatties made of bamboo work, are fastened to an axle, which by revolving with great velocity blows the broken membrane from the bean.—The next operation is that of sorting or garbling, by picking out the small pea-shaped bean from the larger ones. This is sometimes effected by a perforated sieve, through the large openings of which the smaller beans pass, whilst the larger ones remain on the sieve, but much more frequently women are employed to separate the small from the large beans, and at the same time to free them from foreign particles. Some make use of a barrel or sieve made of perforated zinc, of about 3 feet diameter in width, and from 15 to 20 feet long; the perforations are of three different sizes, and the barrel divided into three compartments. It is raised at one end, so as to form an acute angle into which the coffee bean is thrown, and the seed escapes, each size into one of three shallow trays, sorted into three sizes according to the perforations in the barrel. It seems to answer its purpose well.

The coffee is now ready for the market, and is in most

instances transferred to the merchant, for which purpose it is stowed in bags made of the common gunny, of a suitable size, according to the facilities of transit, whether by coolies, pack bullocks, or carts.

CHAPTER X.

Various resources of a Plantation.—In planting operations, whether carried out as Agricultural or Horticultural undertakings, the planter should have an eye to every available product found on an estate, all of which he should if possible convert into money, whereas in most plantations in the present day no attention is paid to the collateral resources, if I may so term them, but the planter looks entirely to the chief product of the plantation, be that coffee, cotton, indigo, &c., without looking to secondary sources of revenue, which arise on every well managed plantation. In coffee planting, the beans are the principal source of revenue, but of late years attention has been drawn to an infusion made from the torrified coffee leaf, which I have manufactured and tried, and was agreeably surprised with the taste and flavour of the beverage so prepared.

Specimens of the coffee leaf tea were submitted to Dr. Hunter, the Hon'ble J. B. Norton, Mr. G. Norton, B. A. Daly, Esq., and a few others, all of whom approved of it except Dr. Hunter, who said, "as far as the flavour was concerned it was a failure, though it had a smell something between coffee and tea."

W. H. Staines, Esq., of Coonoor, states that he has seen and tasted the coffee tea. Attention was first drawn to this subject by Dr. Gardner, in the Great Exhibition. Dr. Gardner submitted specimens of leaves which he prepared from the coffee plant, and proposed their employment as a substitute for China tea. The mode of preparation he protected by a patent.

Subsequently a letter from a Mr. N. M. Ward of Padang

appeared in the Pharmaceutical Journal, Vol. xiii, page 207. Mr. Ward writes from Sumatra, and states that "although familiar with the fact of its being in use among the natives, it never occurred to him that the coffee leaf might be introduced into Europe, until he learnt that a patent had been taken out by Dr. Gardner; the fact of its being the only beverage of an entire population, and from its nutritive properties having become a necessary of life, he considers a sufficient guarantee of its safety as an article of diet, and its freedom from deleterious effects."

"Mr. Ward speaks of his personal experience in the use of the coffee leaf, and further describes the best mode of roasting the leaves, which is by holding them over the clear flame of a fire made of dry bamboo." I have given the coffee leaf tea a trial, and for some time now have been in the habit of using the leaf frequently, and can add my testimony from personal experience. The way I have been in the habit of preparing the leaves, is as follows. The leaves are plucked fresh from the tree, and dried or roasted in a frying pan or other shallow vessel, over a clear fire, and as soon as the leaves attain a brown or buff colour, they are removed from the frying pan and preserved. The only precaution necessary to be used, is to see that all the leaves thrown on the frying pan at one time are of equal size and age, otherwise the more tender leaves are roasted much sooner than those that are more mature, and are likely to be burnt or converted into carbon before the maturer ones have attained the brown colour; the chief principle to be kept in view, is not to roast the leaves too rapidly, and to prevent their getting burnt. By a gradual roasting on a slow fire, the volatile oil or the whole of the Theine contained in the leaves becomes fixed.

I think the plan of roasting in the frying pan superior to that described by Mr. Ward, as practised by the natives of Sumatra, for it affords facilities for roasting large quantities of the leaves at a time, which is a great thing for the planter, as it will save him both time and labour, by enabling him to roast large quantities of the leaves at a time.

The leaves as roasted by me have a faint coffee smell, and ½ an ounce placed in a tea pot and infused with a pint of boiling water, gave a dark brown infusion, with all the appearance of that prepared from the roasted berries, and had a bitterish coffee taste, and with the addition of a little milk and sugar tasted just like weak coffee. Several friends to whom I have submitted samples of the leaves, all agree with me as to the flavour and taste of coffee contained in the infusion, but it does not seem to possess the heating and exhilarating qualities to the same extent as an infusion from the berries, though there can be no doubt but what it exhilarates in a much milder degree. It seemed to me to provoke the appetite and to give vigor to the system; it quenches thirst, and I am of opinion that it will make a pleasant and wholesome beverage, although it may not take with those who are in circumstances to purchase the coffee bean. An extract from the leaf is feasible, and would prove a great boon to travellers; it would at all times be an agreeable drink, from not possessing the stimulating, heating, and appetite impairing effects of the infusion from the roasted berries, and in this country the use of this beverage would obviate the necessity of drinking impure water on the line of march.

It possesses the antiseptic and disinfectant properties of coffee, which will tend to neutralise and purify the ill effects of strange and bad waters. The infusion sweetened with sugar and taken with milk, can be drunk hot or cold at the pleasure of the individual, at all times day or night, to allay thirst. I also believe that it will to a certain extent protect the system from malarious influences, and will do away with that pernicious habit of sipping brandy and water, to which young men in this country are often addicted, under the plea of killing animalcules. Thus whilst the public are supplied with a good and useful drink, the planter will have an additional source of revenue, if he will only take advantage of the knowledge, that the leaves and twigs which now only enrich the dunghill can be turned to account. A large plantation, if properly managed, will supply some thousand tons of coffee leaves without injury, but with even benefit to the plant, by the removal of the leafy twigs which choke up the crown of the plant, owing to the system of topping; these could easily be removed in pruning. The leaves roasted on the spot and bagged, may be sent down for sale or shipped to England.

Even the ripe and yellow leaves which fall from the tree and are of no use to the planter, can with advantage be turned to account. Thus those estates which have failed to fruit, from poorness of soil or climacteric peculiarity, can always be made to yield their leaves with advantage to the planter; and a bad season may thus be partially made up for; according to my experiments, fruit bearing trees will yield annually from 2 to 3 lbs. of good leaves, without interfering with their fertility, and fruitless trees will yield from 5 to 10 lbs. annually. Mr. Ward, in his letter, states, "The price here of the leaves prepared for use is generally *d.*1½ per lb. and I suppose it may be prepared and packed for the European market, of good quality, for *d.*2, affording sufficient profit to the planter, and bringing it within reach of the poorest classes of Europe."

The following extract is taken from an article by John Stenhouse, L.L.D., F.R.S., in the xiii. vol. of the Pharmaceutical Journal, page 382.

"I received from my friend Daniel Hanbury, Esq., a quantity of dried coffee leaves which had been prepared in Sumatra, under the direction of N. M. Ward, Esq., of Padang. The sample had a deep brown colour, and consisted of the leaves of the coffee tree mixed with fragments of the stalks. The leaves had been very strongly roasted in rather a rough manner, and had consequently acquired a slightly empyreumatic odour.

The coffee leaves, when digested with boiling water, yield a deep brown infusion, which in taste and odour closely resembles an infusion of a mixture of coffee and tea. On the addition of milk and sugar it forms a tolerable beverage; and as the roasted coffee leaf can be imported into Europe for rather less than two pence a pound, the poorer classes are likely to find it a very useful substitute for tea and coffee. Should a more moderate temperature be employed in drying the coffee leaf, I think its flavour would be greatly improved. The coffee leaf, as might almost be expected, contains the two characteristic constituents of the coffee bean, viz., theine or caffeine, and caffeic acid.

1. 1,000 grains of dried coffee leaves when treated in the way described, yielded 12·5 grains theine, 1·25 per cent.

2. 1,000 grains of coffee leaves in a subsequent trial gave 11·54 grains = 1·15· per cent.

The amount of nitrogen in the dried coffee leaves was also determined by Will's method 1·344· grm. The substance gave 0·2005 platinum = 2·118 per cent nitrogen.

0·7775 grm. gave 01185 platinum = 2.165 per cent.

Now it has been ascertained as the result of numerous experiments, that coffee contains from 0.80 to 1 per cent of theine, and that tea contains 2 per cent of the same principle, and the nitrogen in coffee beans lies between 2½ and 3 per cent.

From these results it is clear that dried coffee leaves are somewhat richer in theine than the coffee bean, and contain as nearly as may be, the same amount of that principle as Paraguay tea. From the violent roasting to which the coffee leaves had been subjected, I feel convinced that a portion of their theine has been dissipated, and were they only dried at a moderate temperature, I confidently expect that they would yield 1⅓ per cent of theine (its composition is expressed by the formula C. 8 H. 5 N2. O2.)

With regard to the caffeic acid, the other characteristic proximate principle of coffee, the leaf of the coffee plant contains it also in a larger quantity than the berry.

In order to assist in forming an estimate of the comparative value of coffee leaves as a beverage, as compared with the bean, I determined the amount of soluble matter which each of them yielded to boiling water: 6·048 grms. of dried coffee leaves, and 6·038 grms. of roasted and ground coffee beans were repeatedly treated with precisely similar quantities of boiling water, till the liquid which came off from them was nearly colourless. The 6·048 grms. of coffee leaves were found to have lost 2·348 grms. = 38·8 per cent, while 6·038 grms. of roasted coffee beans had lost 1·759 grms. = 29 1 per cent. From this determination it is clear that coffee leaves yield to boiling water near 10 per cent more soluble matter than the bean. In this respect, therefore the coffee leaf has an advantage over the berry."

"So far as regards the two characteristic principles of coffee, namely, caffeic acid and theine or caffeine, these are common both to the leaf and the bean, the leaf being decidedly rich in both. In other respects however they differ considerably. The coffee leaf contains some tannin and scarcely any sugar or fat. The coffee bean contains about 12 per cent of fat, and 8 per cent of cane sugar."—*Philosophical Times.*

Since this was written, and whilst on a visit to the Shervaroys, Mr. Fischer, senior, sent for my inspection some coffee leaf tea manufactured by a Mr. Copp, of mount pleasant Shervaroys. I was agreeably surprised to find that Mr. Copp had manufactured the coffee leaf exactly like the China tea, and had succeeded in the manipulation very well indeed. Mr. Copp was for some time in Assam, where probably he had studied the process of manufacture. I had an interview with Mr. Copp himself, and he gave me three varieties of the coffee leaf tea, which he named successively, "*Orange Pekoe,*" "*Congou*" and "*Souchong*"; the manipulation of these was very good. I submitted a small quantity to the Agri-Horticultural Society of Madras, through Dr. Hunter, and the beverage was curtly pronounced to be *unpalatable.* All innovations in food and drink when first made known are not generally liked, and the same was said of the infused beverages that are now considered indispensable, when first introduced ; but prejudice soon gave way to fashion, the taste was easily acquired, and the beverage found to be healthy, refreshing, and really nutritious, and in these respects coffee leaf tea equals fully the more expensive kinds of infused beverages. I fully believe that if it were brought into more general notice, its introduction as a marketable article would be easily effected.

Some were of opinion that as exertions are being made for the introduction of the China tea (*Thea Bohea*) into Southern India, the introduction of the coffee leaf tea at such a juncture would lead to adulteration, &c., of the genuine tea, &c., but I cannot coincide with this opinion. Coffee leaf tea has already been introduced into England, and from what precedes this, it will be seen that it has been tested in every way by eminent scientific men in connection with the Pharmaceutical Society, and the infusion has been pronounced a nutritious and healthy beverage, well worthy of being introduced more largely for general consumption, so that it requires no recommendation from me.

I have sent specimens of the coffee leaf tea to the Lahore, and hope to send some to the Calcutta Exhibition also. I am about sending a quantity Home. Mr. Copp did not inform me of the process he adopted, but no doubt he followed that practised for the China tea, the manipulation of which I here give.

"**For Green Tea** "—" When the leaves are brought in from the plantations, they are spread out thinly on flat bamboo trays, in order to dry off any superfluous moisture. They remain for a very short time exposed in this manner generally one or two hours ; this however depends much upon the state of the weather. In the mean time the roasting pans have been heated with a brisk wood fire. A portion of leaves are now thrown into each pan and rapidly moved about with the hands. They are immediately affected by the heat, begin to make a crackling noise, and become quite moist and flaccid, while at the same time they give out a considerable portion of vapour. They remain in this state for four or five minutes, and are then drawn quickly out, and placed upon the rolling table and rolled with the hands."

"Having been thrown again into the pan, a slow and steady charcoal fire is kept up, and the leaves are kept in rapid motion by the hands of workmen. Sometimes they are thrown upon the rattan table and rolled a second time. In about an hour or an hour and a half, the leaves are well dried and their colour has become *fixed*—that is, there is no longer any danger of their becoming black. They are of a dullish green colour, but become brighter afterwards."

" The most particular part of the operation has now been finished, and the tea may be put aside until a larger quantity has been made. The second part of the process consists in winnowing and passing through sieves of different sizes, in order to get rid of the dust and other impurities, and to divide the tea into the different kinds known as twankey, hyson-skin, hyson, young hyson, gunpowder, &c.

During this process it is refired, the coarse kinds once, and the finer sorts three or four times. By this time the colour has come out more fully, and the leaves of the finer sorts are of a dull bluish green."

"**Second for Black Tea**.—When the leaves are brought in from the plantations, they are spread out on large bamboo mats or trays, *and are allowed to lie in this state for a considerable time.*"

"If they are brought in at night they lie till next morning." "The leaves are next gathered up by the workmen with both hands, thrown into the air, and allowed to separate and fall down again. They are tossed about in this manner, and slightly beat or patted with the hands, for a considerable space of time. At length, when they become soft and flaccid, they are thrown into heaps *and allowed to lie in this state for about an hour or a little longer.* When examined at the end of this time, they appear to have undergone a slight change in colour, are soft and moist, and emit a fragrant smell."

"The rolling process now commences. Several men take their stations at the rolling table and divide the leaves amongst them. Each takes as many as he can press with his hands, and makes them up into the form of a ball. This is rolled upon the rattan worked table and greatly compressed, the object being to get rid of a portion of the sap and moisture, and at the same time to twist the leaves."

"These balls of leaves are frequently shaken out and passed from hand to hand, until they reach the head workman, who examines them carefully to see if they have taken the requisite twist. When he is satisfied of this, the leaves are removed from the rolling table and shaken out upon flat trays, until the remaining portions have undergone the same process. In no case are they allowed to lie long in this state, and sometimes they are taken at once to the roasting pan."

"The next part of the process is exactly the same as in the manipulation of green tea." "The leaves are thrown into an iron pan, where they are roasted for about five minutes and then rolled upon the rattan table."

"After being rolled, the leaves are shaken out thinly on sieves, and exposed to the air out of doors. A framework for this pupose, made of bamboo, is generally seen in front of all the cottages on the tea hills."

"The leaves are allowed to remain in this condition for about three hours. During this time the workmen are employed in going over the sieves in rotation, turning the leaves and separting them from each other: a fine dry day, when the sun is not too bright, seems to be preferred for this operation."

"The leaves having now lost a large portion of their moisture, and having become considerably reduced in size, are removed into the factory." "They are put a second time into the roasting pan for three or four minutes, and taken out and rolled, as before."

"The charcoal fires are now got ready, and a tubular basket, narrow at the middle and wide at both ends, is placed over the fire; a sieve is dropped into this tube, and covered with leaves, which are shaken on it to about an inch in thickness. After 5 or 6 minutes, during which time they are carefully watched, they are removed from the fire and rolled a third time. As the balls of the leaves come from the hands of the roller, they are placed in a heap until the whole have been rolled."

"They are again shaken on the sieves as before, and set over the fire for a little while longer. Sometimes the last operation, namely, heating and rolling, is repeated a fourth time; the leaves have now assumed a dark colour."

"When the whole has been gone over in this manner, it is placed thickly in the baskets, which are again set over the charcoal fire. The workman now makes a hole with his hand through the centre of the leaves, to allow vent to any smoke or vapour which may rise from the charcoal, as well as to let up the heat, which has been greatly reduced by covering up the fires. The tea now remains over the slow charcoal fire, covered with a flat basket until it is perfectly dry—carefully watched however by the manufacturer, who every now and then stirs it up with his hands, so that the whole may be equally heated."

"The black colour is now fairly brought out, but afterwards improves in appearance. The after processes such as sifting, picking and refining, are carried on at the convenience of the workmen," vol. ii, page 236.*

Another source of revenue to the planter will be found in the pulp of the coffee berries, which in Arabia is converted into a pleasant beverage, and as such it would appear to be generally used and to be rendered marketable, but although it is not possible that we can adopt the system in India with advantage, we can turn the pulpy washing to account, for as we have already seen, it contains much mucilage, gum, sugar, &c. This saccharine and mucilaginous property might be taken advantage of, by allowing the mucilaginous washings to undergo the necessary vinous fermentation, and then be submitted to distillation, when it would yield a large amount of spirit.

Mr. J. B. Norton, writes to me as follows on this subject :—

"Another product from coffee not hitherto thought of;

* Vide Blackwood's Magazine, No. ccccliv, vol. lxxv. January 1854, page 89.

was shown me by Mons. Monclair, by saturating the red husks in a pail of water, invariably after they came from the pulper, and letting them steep till fermentation had well set in, he by means of a still produced an excellent proof spirit like arrack, and the pulp and red husk were still good for the manure heap after the spirit had been extracted."

My friend Mr. Morison also tells me that he has without difficulty, with a common still, procured proof spirits from the washings of the coffee berry. One is surprised to think why this fact has not hitherto been taken advantage of by planters, for it is well known that like other fruits the coffee berry in ripening undergoes the familiar change of the starch or fecula becoming sugar, to which it owes its sweetness produced by what is termed saccharine fermentation, all that is necessary is to convert this into vinous fermentation, the product being alcohol and carbonic acid gas, at the expense of the sugar and mucilaginous matter it contains. The process consists in watching the fermentation, and as soon as it ceases distilling off the spirit from the clear fluid left. If this is not carefully attended to, it may under peculiar circumstances run into what is termed acetous fermentation, or the formation of the alcohol into vinegar.

All that is necessary is an ordinary still, or what is better at less expence the common native still, with which every native is familiar, consisting of an earthen or copper pot with head piece and tube, and which the planter will find in every district where arrack is distilled, and perhaps there are few where it is not.

My own experiments are confirmatory of the above statements, and the spirit thus obtained was what is termed raw spirit, which by re-distillation might be concentrated to the degree wished for.

The dried husks of the fruit (that is, when the bean is allowed to dry in the fruit and subsequently husked or shelled) is infused, and the infusion produced from them is used as a beverage by the Arabs. It is known under the name of ***Kahwe*** or ***Kischer***, and as such is greatly esteemed by them, as it is found not to be so heating as that prepared from the bean itself.* I am of opinion that even the dried shell if macerated sufficiently long (from 2 to 3 days) till fermentation sets in, and then distilled, would yield spirits.

Although desirous of doing so, I have not had an opportunity of testing this part of the subject.

Since the above was written, I have made some experiments on the dry pulp husk, and find that when steeped in water until fermentation sets in, and then distilled, 8 oz. of the husk yielded nearly 1 oz. of spirits.

CHAPTER XI.

Aroma.—Much stress has been laid on the aroma of coffee. The best judges have pronounced that the aroma of the Mocha coffee is wanting in the seeds grown elsewhere, and which is generally attributed to locality, soil, and climate, all of which may possibly produce some effect, but it appears to me that a great deal more depends on the time and state of perfection the coffee beans have attained ere they are collected. We have already seen that the Arab planter does not pluck his berries from the bushes, but shakes off the ripest of them by placing mats under the trees and collecting them subsequently as they drop. There is no doubt that there is much in this, for we to know from every day experience that fruits which ripen on the tree eat much more luscious and well flavoured, and no doubt in such cases the seeds also attain their greatest perfection, and consequently must be better flavoured. This can be better proved by analogy, for all planters know that what is termed *jackal coffee* is also held in greater estimation than what is termed planter's coffee. Why should such be the case, when the fruits were the produce of the same plantation and frequently of the same trees? Could such a difference be caused by the berries passing through the intestinal canal of a jackal? But when we remember that the jackal only selects and devours the ripest berries, and that consequently the seeds must have attained the highest perfection, the difficulty is cleared up. This is the only way that it can be accounted for; for most animals are nice in their tastes, and instinct leads them to select the ripest berries, which, when further examined chemically, are found to contain a larger amount of caffeine matter, which at once accounts for their superiority.

Again we know that the Arab planter does not pulp his coffee berries in their fresh state, but allows them to dry in the fruit, thus the seeds are not exposed to the atmosphere when fresh—it is also possible that some portion of the juice of the berry itself is absorbed by the seed in the drying process. Now almost the same thing happens to seed swallowed by the jackal, for not only are the seeds protected from atmospheric influence in the stomach of the animal for at least we may say 24 hours, possibly longer, but when expelled they are further coated with a layer of mucus which protects them for some time longer. I have carefully examined the beans that have passed through a jackal, in their recent as well as dry state, and could always find them covered over with a fine but perfectly impermeable layer of mucus. This becomes gradually destroyed as the seed dries by the action of the atmosphere. In addition to the above causes, we know that the coffee bean improves by keeping. This is a fact that cannot be disputed, daily experience teaching us that the same thing occurs in grains, as the cereals, millets, &c., which if used soon after being harvested, prove irritant and cause bowel derangements, and the cooked grain is devoid of its particular taste, which is fully developed in the well seasoned seed. If for instance we take the new rice as an example, we find that it causes bowel derangements in natives obliged to eat it. Why should this be the case, when there is no apparent difference in the grain? The difference lies in the constituents; the vegetable albumen has not had time to become consolidated, so that the rice is not only devoid of taste, but irritates the bowels: in the same manner the horny albumen of the coffee has not had time to consolidate, so as to develope its peculiar qualities, and consequently is insipid in aroma. But the seasoned bean has only to be roasted, to develope the aroma to its fullest extent, for it is by this process that the fragrance of its essential oil is brought out, by some chemical change that now takes place. But should the bean not be carefully roasted, it is charred or converted into carbon, and it will possess neither flavour nor taste, even if the bean so roasted should be the best Mocha, but the beverage obtained from it will have an insipid muddy taste. Care should be taken in making the beverage itself, to procure that justly famed, delicious, and exhilirating drink afforded by coffee.

I would draw the attention of planters to the observations made on the ripeness of the berry, and of merchants to those on keeping coffee. A stock should be kept for at least twelve months, so as to improve its quality, and give the merchant an opportunity of making a larger profit than he could otherwise do by its immediate sale. I would especially call the attention of young planters to this fact, for it will be found to increase the sale of his produce and the value of his estate. No coffee from a young plantation should be sent into the market before the next season, or if possible not until the third season, when the excellence of the coffee will get the young planter a name which may be the means of making his fortune, or if he should ever be desirous of retiring from his plantations, will find him ready purchasers.

Not only merchants but planters will no doubt take into consideration the loss they will sustain in the shape of interest to their money if they keep coffee longer than usual in stock, which deserves consideration, but young planters should even at such risk endeavour to gain for their plantations a name at the beginning.

CHAPTER XII.

Stock Yard.—Cattle are the unavoidable additions to the plantation, for all agricultural operations are more or less dependant on stock raising, for the manure they supply will prove in time to be the true regenerator of the soil, and at the same time in most localities their products, either by labour or in the production of milk and butter, will prove of essential service to the planter, who should always possess a stock yard to supply manure to the plantation. But in some localities, the want of grazing lands or fodder of any kind frequently obliges the planter to forego the keep of cattle, though there are few localities perhaps where cattle may not be kept, if not in large herds, yet sufficient at least to supply the planter's wants in milk and butter, and in all cases when properly managed, the manure alone will cover all expences leaving out other resources ; but we shall endeavour to make the subject clear by entering more freely into details, by taking into consideration the outlay for stock, and the various resources that are likely to enable the planter to gain a return from this alone. The outlay of 1,000 Rs. for the purchase of live cattle may be considered large in the formation of a new plantation, and may very likely startle the planter at first, but not so when we come to consider the profits likely to accrue from the manure alone, leaving out that of the stock itself, which supplies the planter with milk, butter, and cream cheese, or veal and beef occasionally.

" The primary object of keeping cattle will be the supply of manure alone, and as such, according to " Boussingalt," a milch cow giving 18·8 lbs. of milk per day, voided in the 24 hours above 18 lbs. of urine, or 6,598 lbs. per annum ; of which the fixed alkaline and earthy salts alone would amount to 309 lbs."

"Assuming that the urine voided in the fields is as well applied as that which reaches the tank, and that Boussingalt's estimate is a fair average for the cattle on a farm over head, a farmer who has a stock of 50 cattle, possesses a local source of ammonia equivalent to 1,779·98 lbs. per annum, which, were it fixed by neutralizing with sulphuric acid, would amount to 3 tons 1½ cwt. of sulphate of ammonia."

"But this is not all, for the fixed alkaline and earthy salts contained in the urine of 50 cattle amount to 6 tons 18 cwt., and as they are more efficient as a manure than any other mixture of salts that has yet been contrived, 1½ cwt would be quite sufficient to dress an acre of grain crop or grass,—hence the quantity above stated would dress 92 acres."*

"The solid excrements of oxen and cows have been analysed by Boussingalt (*annales de chimie* T. LXXI *p.p.* 122 et 134.)

	Solid excrement of a Cow.	Do. of a Milch Cow.
Carbon	44· 00	42· 8
Hydrogen	5· 84	5· 2
Oxygen	34· 17	37· 7
Nitrogen	3· 59	2· 3
Ashes	12· 40	12· 0
	100· 00	100· 0
Water	609· 22	610· 3
	709· 22	710· 3

"The composition of the solid excrements of cattle varies

---

* Agricultural Chemistry by Davy and Sheir, page. 231.

considerably with the age of the animal, nature of the food, its condition, temperament, and the amount of labour, exercise, and exposure in the open air it is subjected to, together with many other circumstances."* Thus it will be seen the large amount of manure that will be at the planter's command from this source alone.

A three year old bull that has been browsing on green grass and getting one measure of varagoo (Panicum miliaceum) at nights, passed in the 24 hours between the 10th and 20th of July 1863 (the average of three days.)

Dung	Urine
27½ lbs.	15½ lbs.

When well sun dried, the dung weighed 4 lbs., and on being carefully incinerated in a new earthen chattee, the ash left was 15¼ oz. The 15½ lbs. of urine on being evaporated in the sun, left a sediment of 1½ oz. and 20 grs.

Per centage of composition of the dung and urine of the bull.

DUNG.

	lbs.	oz.
Water lost by drying	23	8
Organic matter	3	¾
Ash.	0	15¼
Total..	27	8

URINE.

	lbs.	oz.	grs.
Loss of water by evaporation.	15	6	220
Sediment	0	1½ &	20
	15	0	0

* Agricultural Chemistry by Davy and Sheir, page. 237.

A milch cow yielding daily two quarts of milk, and fed on green grass, with one measure of varagoo and three measures of rice tour or bran (the average of 3 days), for the 24 hours gave—

Dung.	Urine.
15 lbs.	11 lbs.

A cow 6 months in calf, out to graze in the day and receiving occasionally some straw at night, the average of 3 nights (12 hours only) was

Dung.	Urine.
8 lbs.	7 lbs.

A cow calf 2 years old, browsing on green grass chiefly, passed in the night (12 hours)

Dung.
3½ lbs.

A buffaloe cow 7 months in calf, browsing chiefly on grass, passed in the night (12 hours)

Dung.	Urine.
14 lbs.	15 lbs.

" The urine of the cow contains, according to the experiments of Mr. Brande.

Water	65
Phosphate of lime	3
Muriate of potassa and ammonia	15
Sulphate of potassa	6
Carbonates of potassa and ammonia	4
Urea	4 *

* Davy and Shier's Agricultural Chemistry 1844, page 229,

" Sprengel gives the following analysis of cow's urine in a fresh state ; the animals at the time having the range of a rich pasture.—100,000, consisted of water........ 92,624

Urea along with some resinous coloring matter. ...		4,000
Mucus...		190
Albumen......................................		10
Benzoic acid..	(hippuric acid) combined with potash, soda, and ammonia, forming salts.	90
Lactic acid. ..		516
Carbonic acid.		256
Ammonia......................................		205
Potash...		664
Soda...		554
Sulphuric acid..	combined with soda, lime,and magnesia, forming salts.	405
Phosphoric acid..		70
Chlorine.........		272
Lime...		65
Magnesia.....................................		36
Alumina......................................		2
Oxide of iron................................		4
Oxide of manganese......................		1
Silica..		36
•		100,000

" Food consumed by a cow in twenty-four hours,!.

Articles of food.	Weight in the fresh state.	Weight in the dry state	Carbon.	Hydrogen.	Oxygen.	Nitrogen	Salts & earthy matters.
Potatoes......	15,000	4170	1839·0	241·9	1830·6	50·0	208·5
After grass....	75,00	6315	2974·4	353·6	2204·0	151·5	631·5
Water........	60000	....	....	....	....	......	50·0
Total....	82,500	10485	4813·4	595·5	4034 6	201·5	890·0

• Davy and Shier's Agricultural Chemistry 1844, page 229.

Excretions of a cow in twenty-four hours.

Excretions.	Weight in the fresh state.	Weight in the dry state	Carbon.	Hydrogen.	Oxygen.	Nitrogen.	Salts & earthy matters.
Excrements....	28413	4000·0	1712·0	208·0	1508 0	92·0	480·0
Urine.........	8200	960·3	261·4	25·0	253·7	36·5	384·2
Milk	85·39	1150·6	628·2	99·0	321 0	46·0	56·4
Total....	45152	6111·4	2601·6	332 0	2082·7	174·5	920·6
Total of first part of this Table.	82500	10485·0	4813·4	595 5	4034·6	201·5	889·0
Difference......	37348	4373·6	2211 8	263·5	1951·9	27 0	31·6
* or	....	......	....	....	....	......	† "

We shall for brevity's sake start with say 50 head of cattle. In the scale of cost laid down for opening a plantation, I have given the average at 10 Rs. per head, but to keep on the safe side as well as to be able to procure good brood cattle, we shall say 48 cows and 2 bulls at........Rs. 1,000

Fodder for the year..................................	"	250
Cow shed and calf pens............................	"	200
Salt..	"	5
Ropes, &c..	"	15
Buckets, milk pails, &c..........................	"	15
Cooly for cleaning and scouring cow sheds, &c. ..	"	20
Cow herd at 7 Rs. per month	"	84
	Total. .Rs.	1,589

Deduct outlay for cattle and sheds 1,200 Rs., the annual expense will be Rs. 389.

* Boussingault Ann. de Chemie et de Phys. lxx 136. The weights in this table are given in grammes, 1 gramme = 15·44 grains troy (very nearly.)

† Liebig's Annual Chemistry, 2nd Ed., page 291.

	Rs.	A.	P.
Return by produce, 15 calves annually, say at 3 Rs. each........................	45	0	0
Milk say at 15 quarts per day, or 5,475 quarts per annum, at one anna the quart..........	342	3	0
Total..Rs.	387	3	0.

Which will cover the annual expense, and the manure may be calculated to pay the interest on capital, which it will do handsomely—or we can form a different estimate on a more practical scale of the value of manure.

50 head of cattle will give each day 25 baskets of manure (the baskets being equivalent to 25 lbs. each), for 365 days........................	9,125
Offal and sweepings from the cottage yard and cow house, &c..........................	315
16 women to bring in 6 bundles of ferns or 6 baskets of dry leaves, each day, say 100 baskets each day, for 365 days......................	36,500
Total...	45,940

which will be equivalent to 600 tons of manure of the best description.

By not using ferns, weeds or leaves, &c., in the cow house every day, to absorb the urine, some portion of it is likely to be lost, and therefore in forming an estimate for cattle, the wages for women to bring ferns, weeds, leaves, &c., should be included, and the quantity and quality of the manure will be greatly improved.

For 100,000, trees will be required 50,000 baskets of manure.

100 head of cattle will give each day 50 baskets, which for 365 days will be....................	18,250
Offal from cook and out houses, coolies lines, &c......	730
16 women will bring in 6 bundles of fern or 6 baskets of dry leaves each, per day, say 100 bundles or baskets each day for the year will be	36,500
	55,480

	Rs.
Two cow boys will be required for looking after cattle, one at 5 Rs. and the other at 3 Rs. per mensem, per annum................................	96
200 acres of pasture land will cost 500 Rs. purchase money. The interest on it at 12 per cent........	60
Kist on 200 acres per annum......................	200
16 womens' hire for the year....................	348
Total..	704

1st Year.

To purchase of 50 cattle...........................	1,000
To cow shed and hut for cow boy................	250
To two cow boys' wages, one at 5 and another at 3 Rs. per mensem................................	96
Fodder for cattle at 7½ Rs, per day, or 225 Rs. per mensem..	2,700
Salt for cattle...	12
Ropes for cattle..	24
Manure pit...	100
	4,182

2nd, 3rd and 4th Year.

To two cow boys' wages for 3 years, at 8 Rs. per mensem...	288
Fodder for cattle for 3 years at 225 Rs. per mensem	8,100
Salt for cattle for 3 years at 12 Rs. per mensem....	36
Ropes for cattle for 3 years at 24 Rs. per mensem..	72
Total...	12,678

Profits or returns.

	Rs.
To manure from the cattle, 25 baskets each day for one year will be 9,125 ; for four years will be 36,500 baskets, at 3 baskets for one anna.	760
To 100 calves in 4 years at 10 Rs. per calf.	1,000
To 50 quarts of milk per diem for 6 months in each year, at 2 annas per quart for 4 years.	150
	1.910

In four years, then, the breeder of cattle will have expended 12,678 Rs., and get a return of 1910 Rs., which will give 15 per cent. interest on the capital. All the young bulls should be castrated, and those required for use on the estate should be broken in not only to draw a cart or to work a plough, but also to carry loads on their backs like pack bullocks, thus they will prove extremely useful in many ways on an estate, and those not required should be sent to the nearest market. In these days of railways and telegraph, they may be sent direct to some of the large stations, where they will be sure to fetch a full price.

Should there be more milk than the planter requires, it can readily be converted into butter and sent to the nearest station, or melted into ghee it will readily find purchasers in every village or town.

The ghee will not only supply the planter's kitchen, but can be used for his lamp where oil is scarce or difficult to be procured. It burns well, and gives a good clear flame and bright light.

I know of one instance in which a planter makes 3 Rs. a day throughout the year, with 50 head of cattle, from milk and Butter alone. The cows receive no care whatever and find their own pasture by grazing in the day. If they were better cared for, I am almost certain the return would be double that stated above.

CHAPTER XIII.

Statistics of Coffee.—The following brief items of the history of coffee may prove interesting, not only to the planter but also to the general reader. According to Mahomed el Azariel Jeziri el Hanbali (who wrote in Egypt about A. D. 1587), coffee was found in use at Abyssinia about the middle of the 15th century, by Jemal ed din Abu Abdulla Mahommed bin Saeed ed Dubani, the Kadi of Aden.* 1430, and introduced into Mocha by Sheik Ali Shaduli ebn Omar.* The coffee tree was introduced into Ceylon by the Arabs, before the arrival of the Portuguese.

1652. The first coffee house opened in London.†

1690. Introduced into Batavia and Java by the Dutch.‡

1714 and 15. Introduced into Martinique by cuttings from a tree sent as a present to Louis 14th of France, by the Magistrate of Amsterdam.||

1718. Coffee introduced into Surinam by the Colonists,||

1728. Introduced into Jamaica by Sir Nicholas Louis.||

1730. Introduced into Ceylon by the Dutch.§

1800. Coffee introduced into Sumatra, by a Mr. Campbell.

1808. Duty reduced in the British Colonies.

1823. Cultivation commenced in Bengal, by Dr. Wallich and Mr. Gordon.¶

---

* Balfour's Cyclopædia, 2nd Supplementary volume, page 147.

† Wonders of the W. Indies, by Mrs. Lynch, page 59.

‡ Balfour's Cyclopædia, 2nd Supplementary volume, page 147.

|| Porter's Tropical Agriculturalist, page 54.

§ Balfour's Cyclopædia of India, article coffee.

¶ Royle's Reproductive Resources of India.

Wynaad by Major Bevan, Manantoddy, and Coorg.

Mungerabad........ ... Bahoo Boodeen Hills.. Chickamungalore.	Mysore, introduced 17th century.
Pulney Hills.......... Cochin Hills..........	Malabar.

Travancore.

Tenasserim provinces, no reliable data.*

1825. The first upland plantation formed in Ceylon by Sir E. Barnes.*

1830. (About) coffee introduced on the Shervaroys by M. D. Cockburn, M. C. S.

Residences in which coffee was cultivated in Java in 1840-41.

	1840	1841
	20	20
Number of families destined for the labour	470,673	453,289
Trees which have yielded a crop....................	216,193,894	236,085,600
Trees which have produced the average quantity of a picul of 25 lbs. Dutch.		

	1840	1841
	280	248
Quantity of coffee furnished to the godowns in piculs.	706,258	877,444
Trees according to the reckoning made in the month of March 1841 and 42................	336,922,460	329,898,963*

* Balfour's Cyclopædia of India.

1846. Coffee introduced on the Neilgherries.

1846. Premiums awarded by the Ceylon Agricultural Society to Messrs. Clerihews' and Josias Lambert, for improvements in coffee pulpers.*

1847-48. Coffee panic.*

1855. Samples of coffee exhibited at the Madras Exhibition, from Munzerabad, Mysore, Neilgherries, and Shervaroys: Shervaroy and Mysore coffee gained 2nd class medals.*

1856. Coffee introduced into Darjeeling by Captain Smaller. Home consumption and Revenue of coffee for the years.

Years.	lbs.	£.
1824	8,262,943	420,988
1825	11,082,970	315,809
1828	17,127,633	440,245
1835	23,295,046	652,124
1839	26,789,045	779,115
1840	28,723,735	921,551
1844	31,394,225	681,616
1845	34,318,095	717,871
1846	36,793,661	756,838
1847	37,441,373	746,436
1848	37,106,292	710,270
1849	34,431,074	643,210
1850	31,226,840	566,822
1851	32,564,164	445,739*
1852	35,044,376	438,084

* Balfour's Cyclopædia of India.

Shipments from Ceylon for the following years, with the class of coffee.

1848-49.	Plantation coffee....	210,633
Native	do.	121,215
		331,848
1849-50.	Plantation coffee............	230,866
Native	do.	99,071
		329,937
1850-51.	Plantation coffee...........	197,636
Native	do.	90,274
		287,910
1851-52.	Plantation coffee.....	155,386
Native	do.	152,621
		308,007
1852-53.	Plantation coffee....	208,658
Native	do.	115,451
		324,109*

Crown Lands sold for the purpose of coffee planting during the following years in Ceylon.

1837..................	3,661	Acres.
1838..................	10,401	„
1839..................	9,570	„
1840..................	42,841	„

* Balfour's Cyclopædia of India.

1841	78,685 Acres.
1842	48,533 „
1843	58,336 „
1844	20,415 „
1845	19,062* „

Present (1857) production of coffee throughout the world.

IN THE WEST.

Brazils	300 millions of lbs.
La Guayra and Porto Cabello	30 „
Cuba and Porto Rico	25 „
Costa Rica	10 „
St. Domingo	32 „
British W. Indies	6 „
French and Dutch do.	6 „
Total	409

IN THE EAST.

Java	140 millions of lbs.
Ceylon	56 „
Indian Peninsular	6 „
Sumatra	5 „
Arabia	3 „
Philippine Islands	3 „
Celebes and Siam	2 „
	215
Millions of lbs.	624

* Balfour's Cyclopædia of India.

Consumption of the world* excepting the countries of production, is stated to be as follows.

United States and British America..	170	millions of lbs.
Holland and Belgium..............	125	"
German Custom's Union............	95	"
Other German states..............	46	"
France........................	33	"
Great Britain..................	32	"
Sweden and Denmark..............	20	"
Mediterranean countries...........	20	"
Spain and Portugal................	15	"
Switzerland.....................	13	"
Russia.........................	12	"
Australia and the Cape of Good Hope	6	"
Total..	587*	

On the Jewaddy Hills near Tripatore there is a small patch of coffee cultivation, which is carried on by the natives.

The hills were visited a few years ago by the late Mr. Lewis Blenkinsop, Assist. Conservator of Forests, himself a planter before entering the Conservator of Forests' Department. This Gentleman reported favorably of the state of the trees he saw, and shewed samples of the coffee produced, which were judged by some of the Shervaroy planters equal to the quality of their own.

1858. Greig's pea berry Machine satisfactorily introduced at the St. Sebastian mills in Ceylon.

Coffee.—"This important berry is being extensively cultivated in the high lands of Southern India, and large

* Balfour's Cyclopædia of India.

tracts of country are available for the extension of its growth."

"The amount and value of the coffee exported from India will be gathered from the table subjoined. **1617** (5065) coffee (coffea Arabica)—Mysore, Colonel Onslow."

Known in the market as 'Cannon's Mysore.'

Showing the Quantities (as far as can be ascertained) and the parts of the World from

Years	Whence exported.	United Kingdom.		France.		Other parts of Europe.		America.	
		Quantity	Value.	Quantity	Value.	Quantity	Value.	Quantity	Value.
		lbs.	£	lbs.	£	lbs.	£	lbs.	£
1850-51.	Bengal	28,787	353	691,476	13,137	123	1	..	..
	Madras.	1,728,076	18,105	205,001	2,050	..	..	..	..
	Bombay	2,452,854	43,026	216,627	3,949	..	..	..	..
	All India. ..	4,209,717	61,484	1,113,104	19,136	123	1	..	..
1851-52.	Bengal	3,043	59	336,814	6,458	..	..	..	..
	Madras.	956,537	9,568	398,455	3,985	..	..	..	..
	Bombay	5,364,855	48,802	..	..	..	..	..	..
	All India. ..	6,324,435	58,429	735,269	10,443	..	..	..	...
1852-53.	Bengal.	19,164	372	143,773	2,798	..	..	..	..
	Madras	1,097,760	10,298	885,966	8,636	..	..	136,080	1,215
	Bombay ..	3,127,921	50,359	201,246	2,594	..	..	..	..
	All India ..	4,244,845	61,029	1,230,985	14,028	..	..	136,080	1,215
1853-54.	Bengal.	..	141	..	5,347	..	..	448	6
	Madras. ..	804,033	8,041	497,753	4,978	..	..	..	..
	Bombay	2,214,751	39,548	1,001,905	17,891	..	..	..	..
	All India. ..	..	47,730	..	28,216	..	..	448	6
1854-55.	Bengal.	171,696	3,350	104,384	2,030	6,720	130	..	..
	Madras	771,716	7,717	339,875	3,399	...	..	..	..
	Bombay	2,235,815	27,198	726,594	9,082	37,380	467	..	..
	All India. ..	3,179,227	38,265	1,170,853	14,511	44,100	597	..	..
1855-56.	Bengal	6,608	137	413,252	8,546	..	..	..	..
	Madras.	1,494,542	14,956	1,107,716	11,077	..	..	2,464	25
	Bombay	3,259,688	53,317	566,293	8,761	52,628	861	..	..
	All India ..	4,760,838	68,410	2,087,261	28,384	52,628	861	2,464	25
1856-57.	Bengal.	..	429	..	3,744	..	2,277	..	..
	Madras.	1,810,972	18,132	1,554,319	15,543	241,259	2,413	40	1
	Bombay	3,298,322	51,352	601,742	8,893	734,806	11,169	..	..
	All India ..	..	69,913	..	28,180	..	15,859	40	1
1857-58.	Bengal	8,250	205	70,188	1,451	40,068	829	84	2
	Madras.	1,068,723	10,678	136,614	1,366	61,119	611	..	..
	Bombay	14,303	29,270	629,296	8,039	420,815	5,961	12,117	224
	All India ..	1,091,276	40,153	836,098	10,856	522,002	7,401	12,201	226
1858-59.	Bengal ...	157,164	3,202	415,884	8,511	...	..	..	..
	Madras	3,402,854	33,742	2,055,386	20,032	1,643	16	..	..
	Bombay	1,506,938	20,182	1,701,291	24,722	164,808	2,207	..	..
	All India. ..	5,066,956	57,126	4,172,561	53,265	166,451	2,223	..	..
1859-60.	Bengal.	896	19	456,288	8,595	12,544	153	5,264	109
	Madras	3,831,800	38,793	3,831,984	54,176	..	..	..	..
	Bombay	812,408	9,792	2,837,760	38,005	..	..	19,236	258
	All India ..	4,645,104	48,604	7,126,032	100,776	12,544	153	24,500	367
1860-61.	Bengal. ..	3,108	74	501,760	11,199	336	8	..	..
	Madras	5,124,899	91,148	7,089,441	125,644	20,412	204	..	..
	Bombay	2,122,358	28,427	1,914,213	41,019	..	..	135,975	2,914
	All India ..	7,250,365	119,649	9,505,414	177,862	20,748	212	135,975	2,914

Countries Whither

value of coffee exported from India and each Presidency to all 1850-51 *to* 1860-61.

Exported.						Total exported to all parts.		
China.		Arabian and Persian Gulfs.		Other Parts.				
Quantity	Value.	Quantity	Value.	Quantity	Value.	Quantity.		Value.
lbs.	£	lbs.	£	lbs.	£	lbs.	Tons.	£
..	..	..	..	36,848	453	757,234	338	13,944
..	..	1,254,692	11,377	97,177	1,179	3,284,946	1,466	32,711
381	5	537,451	6,778	7,928	96	3,215,241	1,435	53,854
381	5	1,792,143	18,165	141,953	1,728	7,257,421	3,239	100,509
..	..	..	..	1,974	40	341,831	153	6,557
..	..	1,272,269	11,463	146,377	1,464	2,773,638	1,238	26,480
280	5	227,285	2,435	2,639	27	5,595,059	2,498	51,269
280	5	1,499,554	13,898	150,990	1,531	8,710,528	3,889	84,306
..	..	..	..	73,449	1,043	236,386	106	4,213
..	...	1,668,413	14,896	197,987	1,911	3,986,206	1,777	36,956
603	12	300,823	3,194	12,367	162	3,642,960	1,626	56,321
603	12	1,969,236	18,090	283,803	3,116	7,865,552	3,509	97,490
..	..	..	..	..	1,102	..	..	6,596
..	..	1,835 533	16,472	827,904	8,283	3,965,223	1,770	37,774
..	..	278,502	3,044	277,411	4,908	3,772,569	1,683	65,391
..	..	2,114,035	19,516	..	14,293	..	..	109,761
..	..	44,800	870	55,888	697	383,488	171	7,077
..	..	2,089,656	18,716	477,922	4,779	3,679,169	1,642	34,611
168	2	336,066	4,325	2,471	32	3,338,494	1,490	41,106
168	2	2,470,522	23,911	536,281	5,508	7,401,151	3,303	82,794
392	8	..	..	9,727	190	429,979	192	8,881
..	..	1,757,148	16,679	368,168	3,541	4,730,038	2,112	46,278
2,960	43	148,660	1,854	15,857	206	4,046,086	1,806	65,042
3,352	51	1,905,808	18,533	393,752	3,937	9,206,103	4,110	120.201
..	1,443	..	14	..	1,147	..	..	9,054
..	..	230,410	2,110	1,342,864	12,190	5,179,864	2,312	50,389
...	..	142,677	1,755	14,507	207	4,791,951	2,184	73,376
..	1,443	..	3,879	..	13,544	..	..	132,819
..	..	..	..	11,887	246	130,477	58	2,733
..	..	1,024,741	9,579	1,958,652	18,995	4,249,849	1,897	41,229
..	..	663,416	12,195	3,534	76	1,743,481	778	55,766
..	..	1,688,157	21,774	1,974,073	19,317	6,123,807	2,733	99.727
392	9	..	..	336	7	573,776	256	11,729
..	..	527,453	4,756	1,369,497	12,401	7,356,833	3,284	70,947
..	..	324,892	4,337	66,657	913	3,764,586	1,681	52,361
392	9	852,345	9,093	1,436,490	13,321	11,695,195	5,221	135,037
..	..	..	..	14,896	307	489,888	219	9,183
..	..	688,680	9,246	1,637,222	26,446	9,959,686	4,459	128,660
..	..	181,718	2,433	15,113	203	3,866,235	1,726	50,691
..	..	870,398	11,678	1,667,231	26,956	14,345,809	6,404	188,534
..	..	..	..	1,008	24	506,212	226	11,305
..	..	574,976	9,920	1,425,504	23,564	14,235,232	6,365	250,480
385	8	141,064	1,879	63,770	1,410	4,377,765	1,954	75,651
385	8	716,040	11,799	1,490,282	24,998	19,119,209	8,535	337,436

" The subjoined remarks on coffee planting in Mysore are by Colonel Onslow. According to the traditions of the country, the coffee plant was introduced in Mysore by a Musselmaun pilgrim named Baba Booden, who came from Arabia about 200 years ago, and took up his abode as a hermit in the uninhabited hills in the Nuggery Division named after him, and where he established a Muth or College which still exists endowed by Government. It is said that he brought 7 coffee berries from Mocha, which he planted near to his hermitage, about which there are now to be seen some very old coffee trees. However this may be, there is no doubt that the coffee plant has been known in that neighbourhood from time immemorial, but the berry has never come into general use among the people for a beverage. It is only of late years that the coffee trade of these districts has become of any magnitude or that planting has been carried to any important extent. There is no record of either further back than the year 1822, when the revenue was under contract. In the year 1837, when the country had been some years under British rule the Raja's authority having been suspended in 1832-3, the contract system was discontinued and a duty of one rupee per maund of 28 lbs. was fixed. From that time the production of coffee and duty is duly recorded. In 1843 the duty was reduced to ½ a Rupee per maund on exportation, and in 1849 to a quarter of a Rupee. Together with the reduction of duties, regulations for taking up and holding coffee lands were adopted. At the same time prices continued to rise.

' Cannon's Mysore' (the coffee exhibited) has risen from 48s. per cwt. in 1846-7, to an average of 96s. per cwt., and has fetched so high as 115s.

" Native coffee sold in the country has risen from 1 Rupee per maund of 28 lbs. to 6 and 8 Rupees. The encouragement thus given to coffee planters has resulted in the great extension of planting, the prosperity of the planters, and an increase of revenue to the state."

" Under the contract system the revenue averaged from 1822 to 1832, 4,270 Rupees annually, and from 1832 to 1837, 7,472 Rupees annually. The yearly average during the next six years under the duty system, the duty being 1 Rupee per maund, was 15,238 Rupees on that number of maunds. During the next six years, the duty being half a Rupee per maund, the average yearly produce rose to 52,236 maunds, giving a revenue of 26,118 Rupees yearly. During the next 12 years, that is up to 1861 inclusive, to which time the accounts are made up, the yearly average of produce rose to 346,083 maunds, and the revenue to 86,824 Rupees, the duty having been reduced to a quarter of a Rupee per maund. This short statement serves to shew the good effect of liberal measures"

" More than 30 years ago a few Europeans were engaged in coffee planting near Chickmoogloor, a few miles from the Baba Booden Hills. About 20 years ago the plantations producing the well known coffee called ' Cannon's Mysore,' and others on the ' Menzerabad mountain,' were commenced by two enterprising gentlemen. The success of these has induced many more Europeans to plant coffee in Mysore. The consequence is, that the coffee trade of Mysore bids fair to emulate that of Ceylon. It has also given an example to other parts of India, and the plant originally taken from the Baba Booden Muth is now extending over tens of thousands of acres in Coorg, the Wynaad district, the Neilgherry hills, and along the Western Ghauts, North and South."

" In Mysore the number of European coffee planters has within the last 10 years increased to 20 or 30. The number of native planters is estimated between 3,000 and 4,000.

" The quantity of land planted or taken up cannot be ascertained with any degree of accuracy. The revenue depending on the quality of the coffee produced, not upon a tax on land, there is no regular correct system of land measurement. This way of taxing is bad ; it leads to bad cultivation and smuggling. It is to be hoped that a land tax will be adopted instead, which would have a good moral and fiscal effect."

" It would put an end to smuggling, and would be a great inducement to the natives to improve their cultivation, which is now very slovenly. If the tax were on the land, they would make more effort to increase the produce of it. The average produce per acre in Mysore is probably not half that of Ceylon."

" The coffee districts are confined to the region of the Western Ghauts and the Baba Booden Hills. Some attempts have been made to cultivate coffee in the open country, but without success ; it seems to require forest land and considerable elevation and moisture. 'Cannou's Mysore' is grown on a range of hills from 3,500 to 4,000 feet above the sea, having the benefit of the South West Monsoon, which very seldom fails at all, never entirely, and of the tail end of the N. E. Monsoon. It is probably to these advantages that the peculiar qualities of 'Cannon's Mysore' are attributed ; viz the closeness of texture and richness of flavour. This elevation gives a pleasant climate well suited to Europeans. During the South West Monsoon, the planter may be in his gardens all day long, without oppression in the hottest weather ; the thermometer in the house on these plantations, rises no higher than 81° or 82° Fahrenheit. The whole of the coffee district, with here and there an exception of feverish spots, possesses a climate in which the European can live and work with comfort, and, with moderate care and prudence, with health."

" Planting has of late years been carried on to such an extent by Europeans and Natives in Mysore, that but little available land remains. These mountain and forest wastes have been turned into rich productive gardens."

" From being the most wild and desolate parts of Mysore, these districts have become very prosperous, and the people have been raised from poverty to comfort, and in many instances to wealth. The Natives are benefiting largely by the capital and example of European planters, and are learning the science of planting. Mysore generally, especially the coffee districts, affords a most promising field for European capital and enterprise."

" 1618 (10,583), Coffee,—Salem,—Messrs. Fischer & Co."

" 1619 (10,749) Coffee in husk—Mangalore." V. P. Coelho, Esq.

" 1620 (6423) Coffee—Chota Nagpore—M. Liebert."

" 1621 (6422) Coffee do."

" 1622 (6567) Coffee—Chittagong."

" 1623 (6098) Coffee—Bombay."

" 1624 (6387) Coffee—Malacca—Captain Playfair."

" 1625 (4771) Coffee in husk (C. Arabica) Burmah, Messrs. Halliday, Fox and Co."

" 1626 (4174) Coffee—Penang."

" 1627 (6699) Coffee—Singapore, W. J. Valborg, Esq."

" 1628 (4171) Coffee—Penang."

" 1629 (4148) Coffee do."

The above is taken from the "Classified descriptive Catalogue of the Indian Departmeut of the International Exhibition of 1862," by J. Forbes Watson, M. D., &c.

LIST OF COFFEE PLANTERS ON THE SHERVAROY HILLS.

Name of Planter.	Name of the Estate.	Where located.
J. Fischer, Esq....	....	Gundoor.
Do.	....	Yercaud.
Do.	....	Vassumbady.
Do.	....	Groondumbady.
Do.	Ballimond........	Green Hills.
*Mr. E. Urilla....	....	Yercaud.
„ W. Lewis	....	Do.
„ G. R. Mayers..	....	Do.
Mrs. Lechler......	....	Do.
Mr. R. Martin....	....	Do.
Mrs. W. Martin ...	....	Do.
Mr. C. McFarlane..	....	Do.
J. Gravier, Esq....	Silistria	Do.
Do.	Hermitage	Do.
Modeen Saib	....	Do.
*G. Richardson, Esq.	....	Do.
* Do.	Balmadies........	Green Hills.
*Genl. Ottley	....	Vassumbady.
Mr. B. A. Daly.. ..	....	Orluncaud.
„ F. Rencontre...	....	Yeechencaud.
„ R. Hurlock. ..	Highfield	Green Hills.
„ C. Grant	Cragmore........	Do.
„ W. Clarke....	....	Do.
L. Ricketts, Esq. ..	Carara	Narthenchet.
Do.	....	Keeleecoor.
Mr. J. Freeman ..	....	Do.
J. B. Norton, Esq..	....	Nagalore.
J. Miller, Esq.	....	Do.
Captain Short....	....	Do.
C. Dale, Esq......	....	Putteebady.
Arnachellum Acharry.......	....	Green Hills.
Mr. Manuel	....	Do.
Do.	....	Putteebady.

* These plantations have passed into other hands, since this was written.

Shervaroy Hills.—*Soil.*—" In forest cleared land on the slopes of hills, and in the deeper valleys, the surface soil consists of a dark vegetable mould, of considerable depth, and in soil of this description the coffee plant luxuriates."

" The soil rests generally upon a reddish clay, which latter appears to have resulted from the decomposition of the surface rocks and laterite covering them. In the more open parts of the hills, the soil is of a light brown colour, and shallower, resting on a similar sub-soil to that previously noticed."

" The coffee and tea plants find their natural home in the soil and climate of these hills, and a few words on the more important productions of hill cultivation may not be out of place here."

" *Coffee.*—The coffee plant was naturalized in these hills about 40 years since, by M. D. Cockburn, Esq., late of the Madras Civil Service, who during his official connection with the Salem Districttook great interest in developing the resources of the Shervaroys. Mr. Cockburn planted several acres of land, and the original trees are still in existence, some of them of large size and capable of yielding when in bearing, 25 lbs. of cleaned coffee. The age at which the fruit bearing powers of the coffee tree cease, is a question of great interest to those engaged in its cultivation. The trees here alluded to are some of the oldest in the Presidency, and they evince no symptoms of decay. The practice of lopping the central shoots about 5 feet from the ground and keeping the plants as bushy as possible, is generally followed here."

" Some of the coffee plantations are kept in very good order, particularly those belonging to Mr. Fischer, the Zemindar of Salem. But most of them are overrun by noxious weeds, balsams and a white passion flower, the fruit of which is eaten by jackalls, and the seeds are thus scattered far and wide. This flower appears to have been originally introduced as a garden plant, but has now gained so firm a hold on the soil, that it has become the coffee planter's greatest pest, and unless all the land owners unite in efforts to exterminate it, the task will soon be an impossible one. Of the influence of this noxious vegetation on the sanitary state of the Shervaroys, more will be said hereafter. At the present time, there are upwards of 5,000 acres of land under coffee cultivation.

The land is generally obtained from Government on perpetual lease, at the rate of 1 Rupee per acre per annum. The best sites for coffee have long since been taken up, but there is still much jungle or forest land available. The average yield in this locality is said to be less than in the Wynaad or in Coorg. A better system of culture, including the use of manure and pruning, would doubtless tend to the production of heavier crops. Some planters appear to have fallen into the error of supposing that it is better to cultivate 100 acres badly, than half the quantity well. It is no wonder, under such circumstances, that what should be highly cultivated land, is almost more obnoxious to the salubrity of the climate than uncleared land."*

Mysore.—" It is stated that there are nearly 10,000 coffee gardens in Mysore, and that the coffee excise for 1861 was Rs. 68,000, which is 9,000 less than in the previous year, from which it is naturally inferred that the Government tax is evaded and smuggling is on the increase."†

---

* Mr. Cornish on the Medical History and Topography of the Shervaroy hills. Madras Quarterly Journal of Medical Science, vol. 3, p. 317.

† " Madras Times," January 8th, 1863.

NEILGHERRIES.

Extract from Captain Ouchterlony's Memoir to the Madras Government in 1847.

" The coffee is cultivated on the slopes of the valleys, and, to a great extent, about Coonoor and Kotergherry, and even more near to Neddiwuttum to the west. From one plantation, in that quarter, 600 acres produced 250 tons of coffee, which, in 1856, sold in the London market for 70s. the cwt. and some for 78s."*

" Numerous plantation of coffee-trees are scattered about the hills, principally situated on the slopes descending to the plains, where the elevation suitable for the growth of this shrub can be obtained. Until within the last two or three years, coffee-plantations were only found on the eastern side of the hills, but representations of the excellent quality of the berry, and of the advantages attending its cultivation on the Neilgherries, having been made in Ceylon, the attention of the skilful planters of that island was attracted in this direction, and the result has been the opening of several plantations, where I ventured to predict, in a former memoir, that this description of cultivation would sooner or later be introuduced, viz., on the western slopes of the hills, where advantages are offered to the planter, eminently superior to those, the possession of which has, of late years, so greatly enhanced the value and importance of the neighbouring island."

" The chief of all is, the cheapness of labour, a cooly receiving even on distant plantations in the " Koondahs" 4 Rupees a month, while in Ceylon, 8, 9 and even 10 are given ; while in the pay of artizans such as carpenters, sawyers, masons, &c., a still greater disparity exists in favor of

* The Neigherries by W. H. Smoult, Esq. 1857, page 95.

this district Second to this is the abundance of labour which can always be commanded here, the neighbouring provinces of Malabar, Mysore, and Coimbatore supplying coolies in sufficient numbers to meet all demands, and at all seasons of the year ; while in Ceylon the utmost difficulty is experienced, in most parts, to obtain labourers when urgently required ; and at all times the supply of coolies is extremely precarious. Planters here have also the advantage of a good public road, passing through the heart of the forest land of the "Koondahs," and affording ready means for obtaining supplies, machinery, &c., or of sending away produce for shipment by a route, of which less than 30 miles are by land and 36 by water, to the port of Calicut. One estate which was opened about 2 years ago near "Wallahkadoo," half way down the Koondah ghaut, by the late Archdeacon of Ceylon and Mr. Hutson, also of that island, and which I had an opportunity of inspecting recently, on my way up from the western coast, is in a very flourishing, condition, and has every promise of turning out most successfully. In its neighbourhood are tracts of virgin forest land of immense extent, stretching away over the innumerable spurs and valleys into which the Koondahs are broken as they slope downwards towards the Ponany river, all eminently suitable for coffee planting, having the proper elevation, a good and rich soil, and enjoying a climate particularly favorable to the nourishment of this peculiar shrub. If the success which is looked for crowns the exertions and adventure of the first speculators, there can be little doubt that when the Koondah coffee appears regularly in the market as a production of this district, the attention of capitalists at home will be directed to it, and the western portion of this mountain tract become a source of great increase to the revenue of the country, while it will afford employment and subsistence to the many indigent people in the neighbouring provinces, who, at the present time, suffer such privations from the want of it, between the seasons of sowing and reaping the crops in the plains, and indeed for more than three quarters of the year."

"The other, or what may be called the old plantations in the other parts of the hills, but principally on the north-eastern slopes, are insignificant in point of size, but remarkable for the peculiarly fine flavour of the coffee produced, which is considered to be owing to the high elevation at which most of them are situated Some plantations near Coonoor and Kotergherry, are 5,000 feet above the level of the sea, but it seems to me that the advantage derived from this superiority of flavour is more than counterbalanced by the general want of vigour and luxuriance of the coffee-trees, which evidently do not thrive in this latitude so well at an elevation above 4,500 feet, as between that and 3,000 feet."

"It is not easy to estimate the amount of land at present, under actual cultivation for coffee on the Neilgherries, as in most cases, the coffee-fields are so mixed up with the mulberry-grounds, that it is difficult to arrive at the precise extent of each, but it may be pronounced not to exceed 280 acres on the eastern side, and 300 acres on the western."

"The general return of those on the eastern side, which are the only ones at present in bearing, is on an average about 6 to 7 cwt. per acre; which is a remunerative rate under the prevailing circumstances of cheap labour, but the trees require manure to keep them up to this rate of bearing and more care in pruning and managing than is bestowed on them."

The above has been taken from "The Neilgherries in 1857, by W. H. Smoult, Esq., see Appendix page 60."

A LIST OF COFFEE ESTATES WITHIN 10 MILES OF COONOOR BRIDGE.

Names.	No. of acres planted.	No. of acres unplanted.	Remarks.
W. H. Staines, Esq.	250		
T. Staines, Esq	150		
Col. Woodfall	150		
Revd. Mr. Wart....			
Mrs. Hayne	100		
J. Hayne, Esq.	50		
R. Groves, Esq....	50		
F. Groves, Esq.....	100		
H. G. Dawson, Esq.	150		
Captain Fuller.. ..	50		
Mr. Sanderson			
Major Sweet.... ..	... .	150	
Captain Hodgson ..	50		
G. McIvor, Esq	....	200	
W. H. Staines, Esq...	100		
Chambers, Esq.. ..	100		
Hunter, Esq.... ..	....	200	
Mullally, Esq......	100		
„ Jun.......	....	150	
Fletcher, Esq......	80		
Aboo Sait, Esq.			
Abdul Cawder			
Nungaparoo	50		
Mr. Butcher.... ..			
M. A. Facien.....			

KOTAGHERRY ESTATES.

Aboosait ....Sailhara.

Fletcher....................Anatooray.

Colonel Browne......... ....Bolbara.

Strange................ ....Riggerbunner.

Cockburn 1............ ......Cunconypetty.

——— 2............. ....Heesoovay.

——— 3.............. ..Gooday Gulloo.

Fraiser and Tuille ....Arma Cutten.

Colonel Cooper................Tetapollum.
Arbuthnot.............. ....Tenagarda.
Framjee and Ryall ....Davahutty.

Coorg.—" A few particulars of the coffee estates in the Coorg country.—Veerajendapett is situated between Mercara and Cannanore, 50 miles from the latter place and 20 from the former. This new but highly favored district, is now commanding the attention of all whose minds lean towards coffee. " Wild wastes" are disappearing ; smiling cultivation abounding on all sides. Everlasting verdure, grace, majesty of form, height, and amplitude of growth, are the distinguishing attributes of forest trees. The elevation is 3,500 feet above sea level, but there is forest land situated 5,000 feet and upwards. The general aspect of estates is Eastern. Cooly labour is abundant. The rate of labour for *able bodied* men is 5 rupees a month, excepting for about two months in the felling, season, when "SUPERIOR" men get 6 rupees for doing *axe work* ONLY. The first settler is a Doctor Maxwell, in the neighbourhood of Perimbady. His labours are now being crowned with success. His estate has many advantages in the way of situation over other plantations. In the same neighbourhood are the estates of Messrs. McGregor and Brown. The former gentleman a Ceylon planter of great experience."

" Nearer to " Veerajendapett," a place famous in Indian history, are the estates of Mr. George Anderson. " Woodside" is second to none in Coorg. This estate is now giving its first crop. To the energy and ability of the proprietor, its success is in a great measure due. Mr. Anderson's assistant is a Mr. Blandford."

" There are also the estates of Mr. D. Rose, Mr. H. P. Minchin, Mr. J. Stewart, and Mr. Donald Stewart, " *The planter*" of Coorg. The latter gentleman has great possessions, and was formerly a Ceylon planter. To him are due the best thanks of the community, for his willingness at all times to impart information. Mr. Stewart is much esteemed and respected by all."

"Coffee estates are now being formed at and around the German Mission station at Anandapoor, situated 8 miles from Veerajendapett. The neighbonrhood, although not possessing the heavy forest land which abounds elsewhere, is well spoken of. It is partly forest and Bamboo soil. The Anandapoor estate is a standing evidence of what may be done in coffee growing in this locality. Captain James, Mr. J. P. Hunt, and Mr. Gillibrand, have lately settled in the neighbourhood of Anandapoor, and are well pleased with their prospects ; labour abundant and cheap: sufficient rain fall, and elevation good."

"The natives of Coorg are daily opening their eyes to the profits derived from coffee cultivation, and it is not uncommon to see their threshing floors for rice filled with coffee."

"Little however can be said in favor of these consumers of betel mixture— whether it is that the mildness of the climate and fertility of the soil render active exertion unnecessary, but these people seem to regard *sloth* as the chief luxury. Jungles have risen to an enormous price. Forest which might have been purchased 2 years ago for 1,500 Rs., is now valued at least six times that amount. But the lease of these cardamom Jungles expires in three years, and unless the greater portion is under proper coffee cultivation, Government will put the same up to auction, and the highest bidder obtains. Some Coorg Natives are insane enough to suppose that if they put in seed coffee on the ground, regardless of the wood or underwood being cut, that they will be in such a case entitled equally with the European planter to hold their jungles *as* coffee *plantations* ; but surely Government wont be taken in by such a silly trick. Almost daily, exceedingly fine offers for jungles are made by Europeans to these Coorgs, but they will accept nothing in reason. The cardamoms scarce pay their rent to Government. It is altogether a dog in the manger case. But who can sympathise with these people by and bye, when opposed at auction by the Europeans."*

† Dr Bidie speaks thus of the climate and flora of Coorg, and its suitability for Cinchona cultivation, as his observations are equally applicable to coffee, I give them in full.

" Coorg is the central portion, the great mountain chain that separates Malabar from Mysore and the Carnatic, and varies in elevation from 3,500 to 4, 500 feet above the level of the sea. Its climate is remarkable for its great perennial humidity, its heavy rain fall varying from 100 to 150 inches, and its cool equable temperature ranging from 55° to 75°. It may be said to be entirely covered with dense lofty forest, except the small portions cleared by the coffee planter and farmer. The soil throughout is a vegetable mould, generally resting on decayed primary rocks rich in felspar. The larger forests on the slopes of mountains in gorges are characterized by Myrtaceæ, Artocarpaceæ, Ebenaceæ, Guttiferæ, Enonymus, Canarium, Calophyllum, Dillenia, Lagerstræmia, Myristaceæ, Cinnamomum, Cedrelaceæ, Michelia, Monosis, Polygaleæ, Araliaceæ Areca, &c., and in their shade we have numerous, Orchids, Cardamoms, two species of Callamus and Piper. In more open parts we have Melastomaceæ, Ardisia, Rubus, Rosa, Callicarpa, Bamboos, Artocarpus, Jasminaceæ, Salix, Toddalia, Vaccinum, Caryota tree and other ferns, Lycopodiaceæ. &c., characteristic of the vegetation."

* Peoples' Almanac for 1863.

† Madras Quaterly Journal of Medical Science No. xiii, July 1863, page 156.

"In judging of the fitness of a place for the culture of Cinchona, we must consider the nature of the soil and of the rock formation, the temperature and humidity of the climate, the elevation, and the characteristics of the local flora. Undoutedly the most reliable data are to be gained from the characteristics of the local flora, as constant relations exist between the flora, and the climate and geological formation of the country. On the other hand, nothing can be more unsafe as a guide than the mere elevation of a district, for we find plants growing say at 3,000 feet on the Eastern flanks of the Coorg mountains, which would not live through a single season at the same height on their Western slopes, and while in one range of hills in India the temperature diminishes at the rate of 1° for every 300 feet of elevation, on the Neilgherries the proportion is 1° for every 340 feet, and in Khasia but 1° for every 380 feet, Again on the Andes the range of low land cultivation extends to nearly 6,000 feet above the level of the sea, while in Teneriffe it does not exceed 3,000 feet, and in Southern India it certainly does not pass 4,000 feet."

"Impressed with these facts while investigating the flora of Coorg, the conviction was borne in upon me that although at a mean elevation of but 4,000 feet above the sea, I was nevertheless surrounded with a vegetation identical in its leading features with that of the bark districts of South America. There the characteristic plants are said to be tree ferns, palms, gigantic climbers, Bamboos, Plantains Aroidæ, Cecropias (Artocarpaceæ) Melastomaceæ, Myrica, &c., and in the open part of Coorg, a similar flora of which we have already spoken prevails.- The next questions that arose in my mind, had reference to temperature humidity and soil. In the region of the Cinchonas, the mean temperature ranges from 62° to 68° and the humidity is said to be excessive. In the higher parts of Coorg, the mean temperature is from 65° to 68°, and these vast forests of which we have spoken give sufficient evidence of great perennial humidity of atmosphere. As to the soil and geological structure they agree exactly with those of the Cinchona zone of the Andes, where the soil is chiefly a vegetable mould and the rocks of primary formation and rich in felspar."

"The District of Coorg which I consider especially suited to the cultivation of Cinchona, may be said to extend from the Brummagheries in the South to Mercara in the North, and from the crest of the Ghats on the West to the longitude of Anandapoor on the East."

"At present all the better parts of the land on this tract are being secured by coffee planters, and in a few years, if matters go on as at present, the greater portion of it will be under coffee. If therefore I may be permitted to offer such a suggestion, I would strongly impress on Government the necessity of at once securing as much of it as may be considered necessary for Cinchona plantations, for the districts in India suitable for such are neither numerous nor extensive, and the day is certainly approaching, when we must be dependant on our own resources for a supply of the priceless bark—Hoonsoor 25th April 1863.

The Produce of an Acre, or individual Plant.—Desirous of ascertaining the largest crop produced by a single plant, I applied to several Gentlemen for information. From 7 to 15 cwt. the acre, is considered a large crop by many planters, and plantations have been known to yield 15 cwt. According to Mr. Smoult's statement with reference to the Neilgherries already referred to, the produce of an acre will approach 1,000 pounds. General Ottley considers that an average yield of 4 lbs. of marketable coffee from 10 year old plants very good, and I believe the General has realized at this rate on some of his plantations. Mr. Edwin Urilla on the Shervaroys states, that on more than one accasion he has realized on Mr. Richardson's estate 25lbs. of marketable coffee from a single plant. The plant was said to stand between 15 and 20 feet in height, and the locality where it stood was pointed out to me.

Mr. G. Copp of Mount Pleasant, Green Hills, Shervaroys, tells me that he has taken off, for 6 or 7 years running, 25 and 7 lbs alternately from a single plant, which he pointed out to me, and which I examined. It stood between 10 and 12 feet in height, next a rivulet or hill stream, and I certainly never saw a coffee tree better covered with young fruit; the branches seemed groaning with the load; the tree appeared to me to be about 10 years old.

A Mr. W. Orphwood, who was one of the first settlers on the Shervaroys, assures me that he never realized more than 12 pounds of good marketable coffee from any one plant during an experience of a quarter century.

Coffee Wood.—The coffee wood does not seem to attain any very great girth. The largest I have examined did not exceed a diameter of 6 inches. Mr. Fischer, Senior, tells me that he has seen wood of double the girth I name. The wood is strong and light coloured, hard and close grained, and is generally close jointed, which in a measure adds to its strength. It is greatly prized for wood printing, engraving, and carving. At the school of Arts, Madras, Dr. Hunter shewed me some admirable specimens of coffee wood carving, &c.

The smaller branches are much valued as walking sticks, and as such are in great requisition. I saw bundles of them at Mr. Fischer's at Salem, being polished, which they take very well.

Although the coffee plant requires a particular altitude, with certain conditions of climate and temperature to luxuriate in, yet it will be found not only to thrive, but to fruit tolerably well, in the most opposite localities with moderate care. In a medical topography of modern Orissa, I thus noticed its growth. Coffee would undoubtedly thrive well. I have seen coffee trees in some of the gardens of Cuttack, loaded with fruit, and a few trees in Captain Saxton's garden furnished our supply for the jungles; the coffee is as rich in aroma and flavour, as any I have tasted produced elsewhere."*

In Madras, at 38 Poonamallie Road, there are some 50 or 60 coffee plants growing in the shade. I should say that these trees are now about 14 or 15 years old, and from want of pruning and other care they have grown lanky. They seem to fruit annually tolerably well, and are now in fruit.

At No. 12 Kilpaukum garden road, there are some 40 trees in Mr. A. Walter's garden, which I am told are now in their fifth year, and are pretty well covered with fruit. Mr. Walter states that at Penang the coffee plant appears to grow wild. I believe that coffee is found growing in other gardens about Madras.

I have a few trees at Chingleput. I started with three plants in 1857. One was destroyed during my absence from this place on sick leave.

I have now besides a number of younger plants, all apparently growing well.

---

* Dr. Shortt on the Medical Topography of Modern Orissa, vide Indian Annals of Medical Science vol. 5. page 185.

CHAPTER XIV.

Hints to Planters on the preservation of their health, and that of their Establishment.—The localities where coffee thrives, are generally moist and the climate mild, but from the dense jungles and luxuriant vegetation which so readily spring up on every side, these places are not free from malaria. The constant decomposition of organic matter, not only of vegetable origin but frequently of animal also, soon tends to deteriorate the health of the planter, his superintendent and coolies who in time may become a prey to sickness of such a nature, that if not carefully attended to and skilfully treated, it may terminate fatally.

Another source of danger arises from the dampness and mildness of these localities, which frequently induce Europeans and East Indians to throw aside all ordinary precautions, and expose themselves improperly clothed and at all hours to the open air; frequently sitting when in a state of perspiration in a draught, or taking cold drinks, &c., when heated, and thus bringing to a stand the cutaneous transpiration, by causing congestion of various organs and giving rise to one or other of the following diseases; viz. fever, dysentery, diarrhœa, dropsy, and rheumatism, the latter frequently the sequela of fever. As far as my own personal knowledge extends, these are the most formidable diseases that planters and their servants suffer from.

Patients labouring under these diseases, chiefly coffee planters from Ceylon, the Shervaroys, Mysore, and Wynaad, have come under my own observation and treatment from time to time, so that as I have some experience and can speak confidently on the subject, I should consider myself wanting in duty should I neglect to impress deeply on all planters and their superintendents, that in all cases of sickness, be it ever so trifling, they ought to call in medical advice when within a reasonable distance from their plantation. This is a duty they owe to themselves and their families ; for the planter's knowledge of medicine, if he possesses any, has generally been acquired from desultory reading, and possibly experiment on some too confiding friend or unfortunate cooly, and such knowledge must of course be vastly inferior to that of the medical man, whose study and attention have been directed to the great objects, the prevention and cure of disease. With these preliminary remarks, I shall now enter on that most important and dangerous disease fever, of which there are several varieties on which it is not our purpose here to enter.

The fever common to planting localities generally takes on two forms, the Intermittent and the Remittent, and in almost every instance the former merges into the latter. Now fever may arise from several causes. First from malaria or the inhalation of noxious matters arising from the putrefaction of animal and vegetable matters, and the exhalation from damp ground, from hill streams and freshes overflowing their confines, or it may arise from a chill taken by sitting in the wind when in a state of perspiration, or the taking of cold drinks when the body is heated by exercise, &c. This same cause will produce Dysentery, diarrhœa or dropsy, according to the habit and temperament of the individual and the inherent weakness of his constitution. For instance, sudden check of the perspiration in one person would produce fever, while in another it would produce congestion of the mucous membrane of the bowels, and give rise to either dysentery or diarrhœa, and in a third, debility caused by sudden disturbance of the balance between the exhalents and absorbents, will give rise to dropsy of the flesh or dropsy of the abdominal cavity. In fevers, planters are in the habit of resorting to the use of quinine in large doses. Although I approve of large doses of quinine, and have used it successfully in fevers contracted in the jungles of Orissa, Kamptee, the Shervaroys and Mysore, in large doses of 20 and 25 grs., yet I do not think it prudent to use it in all cases without previous preparation of the system, and various circumstances have to be considered. In some cases the liver may be deranged and will require attention, or there may be much fullness of the vascular system with violent head-ache, or the stomach may be foul, and will require to be cleansed out by a mild emetic or aperient before quinine is had recourse to, nor does it follow that because a dose of quinine cured an attack of ague on a former occasion, it should be resorted to again without a moment's consideration. In dysentery and diarrhœa, attention to diet will be necessary. In dropsy, the bowels and kidneys will require especial attention ; but in all cases it is much more satisfactory to seek proper medical advice at once. It will be found that as long as excessive moisture continues on the ground, fever, dysentery, and diarrhœa will prevail. The planter cannot be too careful of his own health, and that of his establishment—Extreme fatigue of every kind should be avoided. The commencement of the rainy season will frequently be found to be the most sickly time of the year, unless the rains come down in abundance and clear the locality of malaria. The planter or his superintendent and coolies should on no account sleep out in the open air, and when their doing so is unavoidable, large fires should be kindled in the vicinity, so as to protect them from the night air.

Good living is not only necessary but actually essential to keep up the stamina of the system, Care should be taken that the coolies partake of their meals regularly, and on each occasion it should be fresh cooked ; and in places that are reputed to be sickly and where coolies have to be imported from any distance, care should be taken to supply them with animal food once a week if not oftener. The whole of the planter's establishment should as a rule be compelled to retire into their huts ere night fall, and the planter himself should not remain out after that time, and in extremely sickly localities or during the period of sickness all should retire within their dwellings before sun set; the windows and doors should be shut, except a ventilator or two, which should be high up the wall, as close to the roof as possible.

The same rule should be practised in the morning, not to leave the cottage before sun rise, and then on no account to do so with an empty stomach, something solid should be partaken of; a cup of strong coffee and a crust of bread is the best thing that can be taken. The planter should at all times avoid swamps or other boggy places, and when duty calls him to visit such localities, he should not stay a moment longer than necessary.

Water forms an important item in the diet of man and animals, and the planter cannot be too careful as to the kind of water he makes use of, for disease is often to be traced to the use of bad water. Water should when possible be dug for in sandy or other strata, where by percolation it is likely to be strained of its impurities, and where this is not feasible, Hill streams should be conducted over a strata of sand or gravel artificially created, and the water after passing over this stratum might be made use of, or if this is not covenient, the water should be boiled over night and strained the next morning through some stout calico or flannel, before being made use of.

Europeans cannot be too careful about their health; they should as a rule live well and be warmly clad, wear woollen socks, good stout shoes or ankle boots, and never sleep without mosquitto curtains.

It is equally necessary for natives to be well clothed ; a good woollen jacket or calico padded with cotton, as used by natives in upper India, (the common tree silk cotton answers well) should be worn ; they should be furnished with straw or dry grass to sleep on, or what is better a charpoy for each cooly, or an earthen mound about 4 feet high within the hut, should form his cot, and great care should be taken in the selection of coolies, to avoid those who are sickly or out of health. With these simple precautions a man may retain his health on a plantation even in the most sickly localities.

INDEX.

Page: